Tragedy
of the
Reformation

Journeys of Faith®
1-800-633-2484
Bob & Penny Lord

Other Books by Bob and Penny Lord

THIS IS MY BODY, THIS IS MY BLOOD
Miracles of the Eucharist - Book I
THIS IS MY BODY, THIS IS MY BLOOD
Miracles of the Eucharist - Book II
THE MANY FACES OF MARY
a Love Story
WE CAME BACK TO JESUS
SAINTS AND OTHER POWERFUL WOMEN
IN THE CHURCH
SAINTS AND OTHER POWERFUL MEN
IN THE CHURCH
HEAVENLY ARMY OF ANGELS
SCANDAL OF THE CROSS AND ITS TRIUMPH
MARTYRS - THEY DIED FOR CHRIST
THE ROSARY - THE LIFE OF JESUS AND MARY
VISIONARIES, MYSTICS AND STIGMATISTS
VISIONS OF HEAVEN, HELL & PURGATORY
TRILOGY BOOK I - TREASURES OF THE CHURCH
TRILOGY BOOK II - TRAGEDY OF THE REFORMATION
TRILOGY BOOK III - CULTS - BATTLE OF THE ANGELS
ESTE ES MI CUERPO, ESTA ES MI SANGRE
Milagros de la Eucaristía
LOS MUCHOS ROSTROS DE MARIA
una historia de amor

Table of Contents

Dedication

This book is about victims, of yesterday and today. It is about tragedy and separation which did not have to be. We must dedicate this book to those who have been most affected by it then, when it happened. We have to look to those who suffered and died because of man's greed for power and wealth, and his complete lack of the milk of human kindness.

In reading this book, you will learn about men and women who fought battles, put their lives on the line and died for their belief or lack of belief in various truths of our Church. You'll read about powers that were given to monarchs and nobility as well as priests and bishops, to slaughter and kill in the name of Jesus. *Their victims are the people to whom we dedicate this book.*

We stood before a Famine Grave in Ireland where tens of thousands of Irish Catholics were buried after being forced to starve to death because someone allowed a maniac to take control of England and Ireland and kill them. This maniac was allowed to take power because of a heretic who began a new religion two hundred years before. *We dedicate this book to those slaughtered victims.*

This book is a sad book. We talk about the events which allowed 40,000 splinters of the True Cross of Jesus to come into existence in order to weaken and destroy the Body of Christ. They are reminiscent of the Jews who wandered in the desert for forty years. These millions of Catholics who are no longer Catholic because someone gave into the principles of the enemy through the pride of someone we don't even know, *these millions of wanderers are the victims. We dedicate this book to them.*

This book is about the you and me who are separated brothers and sisters in Christ through no fault of our own. We cry hard tears for us because we are so many worlds apart regarding a difference in how we believe in God and how we adore Jesus. We can't find a common ground and our leaders, priests, bishops, ministers, patriarchs are too involved in matters of consequence to care what happens to the rank and file in their Church or in any Church. *We are victims; we yearn to be together. This book is dedicated to us.*

Finally, this book is dedicated to those who care. We include our Pope, our Cardinals and Bishops who are in union with His Holiness in an effort to bring back those who were lost, to find the lost tribes of Israel, our separated brothers and sisters in Christ. We dedicate this book to caring Catholics and Protestants who want to bring us together under the chair of Peter. We dedicate this book to ministries like ours, Mother Angelica's EWTN Catholic Cable Network, other ministries who are trying to keep those who are tottering and bring back those who want to come back. This book is dedicated to Our Lord Jesus Christ, His Mother Mary, our cousins the Angels and our brothers and sisters, the Saints, who weep until we are all joined together. This Tragedy of the Reformation should never have happened. *We dedicate this book to those who will work with their last ounce of strength that it never happens again.*

They Never Knew What Hit Them

My God, how did it happen?

How did 6,000,000 faithful Roman Catholics leave their beloved Church? *They never knew what hit them!* And by the time they realized it, it was too late.

How did it come about, and why has the Lord directed us to write this book *now*? The loyalty that many of our precious brothers and sisters in Christ have for their religions is the same kind of loyalty and faithfulness that their ancestors had for the Catholic Church. Many of our separated brethren remain where they are because of relationships with their wonderful pastors or because of family ties. Imagine the pain of their beloved ancestors when they discovered that the priests that they had trusted had led them out of the Catholic Church! *Or did they ever find out?*

How many today believe that they belong to a church founded by Christ? This book is not about contests, who is right and who is wrong, but about unity! May Our Lord Jesus Who died for us all, touch the hearts of everyone who reads this Trilogy we have written. We need one another. The enemies of Christ are united; we must be united! We can still hear Our Lord Jesus crying out to His Father for us all to be one, as the Father is in Him and He is in the Father.[1]

With each book we write, we feel ourselves coming closer to what we believe the Lord is saying to us, like pieces of a puzzle coming together. When we wrote our first book[2] we never suspected it would be used to defend the Real Presence of Jesus in the Eucharist! How were we to know that this would then lead us to research and write about Mother Mary, the Saints, the Angels, and the Martyrs? Was it to give us role models to help us live in this troubled world?

The more we wrote, the more the Mystical Body of Christ reached out to us and shared their joys and hopes, but mostly their hurts and fears. As we got to *know* our Heavenly Family more, we began to *love* our earthly family more. We discovered that we are not alone. We, the Church Militant, linked to the Church Suffering, to the Church Triumphant,[3] are all together, forming a powerful army armed with God's Grace to fight the good fight!

A love affair started in 1975, in our hearts and minds that has grown to a passion - to live and die for our Church. We want to shout from the mountain tops: *Jesus is the Way, the Truth and the Life*, and this His Church is the visible manifestation of *His Way*, *His Truth and His Life*. His Love ever present to us in His Word, on the Altar and the Tabernacle, He is there for us to follow. It's such a grand Church with such a great heart, big enough to love all the children Jesus left her at the foot of the Cross.

The more we studied, the more we found ourselves hungering to know our *Church* more, what had gone before, the battles waged and won, the heroes and anti-heroes - for the last 2000 years. Each controversy fought and won gave us hope when everything looked hopeless, strength when all felt helpless, encouragement in the face of discouragement, onward vision and determination when all around us wanted to give up. A light came into our lives drowning out the darkness, and we discovered that light - Who was *the Light* - through our Church and suddenly we knew we could make a difference. As the years flew by, sorrowful tears were replaced by tears of joy, as we knew that Our Lord and His whole Heavenly court were there beside us, reassuring us, filling us with His Peace.

We could never have anticipated that the hierarchy and religious of our Church would accept our writings, but they proved us wrong. We had written solely with Catholics in mind, never daring to hope that our *separated brethren* would read our books and newspapers, no less watch our programs on EWTN.[4] But again *they* proved us wrong with not only members of our non-Catholic family calling us but their pastors as well. Then we knew: it is not what we believe that separates us but *that which we do not know* - God always the Revealer, the Truth setting us free, and Satan the concealer trying to keep us in the dark with him - lest we believe and are set free.

It has taken us eight years to write this Trilogy. The Lord gave us this thought many years ago, but we have discovered that the Lord often gives us *first* His plan and then years later He reveals the timeframe. Experience has taught us that it is essential we wait for *His* timetable, the waiting although painful at times is nothing compared to the pain realized when we try to push God's plan into happening ahead of His schedule. *Lord give us always the strength and wisdom to live Your Will according to Your timetable.*

What happened to Mother Mary? Since my earliest childhood,[5] I have had an ongoing love for our separated brethren; therefore whenever I learned someone had converted to the Catholic Church, I had a hunger to discover how, what and why he/she had come Home to Jesus' Church! In years past, the answer was always: *the Eucharist, Jesus alive in our Church*; but when I would bring up Mother Mary, I would either see a cloud form over the joy that had filled our sharing, or a veil covering his/her eyes or worse a flat rejection of Mother Mary. After we wrote our book on Mother Mary[6] we began to hear from converts who, eyes shining, were proclaiming that it was *Mother Mary* who had led them to her Son in the Eucharist and to the only Church where He dwells - in the Tabernacle and on the Altar. They had come into the Church with the arms of Jesus' Mother leading them. She had won their hearts. They discovered she was the Mother they had been seeking, and rather than lead them to herself and away from Jesus, she was the bridge that was leading them to His Way, His Truth, His Life. They wanted to know more about Mary - *Daughter of the Father, Mother of the Son,* and *Spouse of the Holy Spirit* - how at times of crisis, we have her ongoing involvement in our lives and in the life of the Church.

We have always considered ourselves converts. When we lost our beloved son at age 19, we left Jesus and His Church. When we came back to Jesus and the Catholic Church three years later, we had an urgency to find out how we could have walked away from Our Lord and the precious Church which flowed from His Sacred Heart on Calvary. We have spent almost 23 years searching for the answers.[7] All our books have taken us on a journey through the history of our Church, the Lord guiding us book by book to the truth that *This is His Church and we should treasure her*.

We discovered that we were the Mystical Body of Christ! What an awesome privilege to be part of Jesus in such an intimate way. For many years, when our brothers and sisters in Christ would ask if we had accepted Jesus as our personal Savior, we would hunger to join them because even without knowing Him deeply - with a synthesis of head and heart, we knew we loved Him and we wanted to be close to Him. When we came back, we knew we had to answer the gnawing question of how we could have left Him and His Church, not only for ourselves but for you.

I remember when we were Sunday and holiday go-to-church Catholics and knew little about our Faith, I would overhear Bob say to the children, *"Don't fill Mama's head with too much. We like the way she believes."* The only problem was that I did not have the *faith* of a child but the *knowledge* of a child, and our Church is an *adult* Church -

one that requires a lifetime of lifetimes of study to even begin to discover the *Treasures* stored in her Heart. Oh, I loved Jesus with all my heart, but I left Him because I didn't truly know Him. After we came back, I knew the only way I would have that personal relationship with Jesus which I had always desired was through the Catholic Church. So we travelled to shrines all over the world seeking and finding Jesus and, with Him, all the many Treasures of this glorious Church. We have such an urgency to share them with you, we write and write and write. The more we have learned about Mother Church, the more we have grown to love her and our Lord Jesus, and you our brothers and sisters.

Now, as I said, God is the Revealer, and do you ever notice how painful revelation can be? As we learned more about the Church and her gifts, delving more deeply into the Deposit of Faith that makes up our Church, we became keenly aware of abuses *within* our Church. Now, our Church is perfect in that she was founded by He Who is perfect, and flowed from His Royal, most precious Heart. But the Lord has always picked imperfect men and women on the way to perfection, to serve His Church; and the enemy of God - Pride has gotten to some of them, leading them to disobedience which in turn leads to dissidence.

The Church is under attack! We were becoming discouraged by some of the things that were happening. The Lord led us to dig deeper into the *History* of the Church and the ongoing attacks on the Church from its infancy until today, the heresies which cropped up and were dispelled, our Church defining conclusively for all times a Dogma we had always believed from the very beginning. As we are writing this Trilogy on the Church, we can see that it is a companion to our book on the Heresies that attacked the Church down through the ages.[8] It is a link to strengthen those within the Church and to enlighten those without who do not know the truth about Mother Church.

Over the last twenty plus years, as we have journeyed deeper into the history of the Church, and especially into the cause of the Reformation, we have discovered the Lord was asking us to put all the pieces of the puzzle together. As we did so, we found that what was evolving was that much of that which attacked our Church from without,[9] came from old heresies which had attacked her from within, and had been dispelled by Councils centuries before. We also discovered that this Trilogy was not only to fortify those within our Church and to call Home those who have left,[10] but to unearth what is happening *within* our Church today. With so many afraid to speak up and challenge the heresies, and disobedience being promulgated by *some* of our own hierarchy, will we have a repeat of the *Tragedy of the Reformation* where millions of Catholics were led out of the Church by heretical priests, bishops and rulers, and did not know they were no longer Catholic? Will we be silent and see our children and grandchildren robbed of the Church which brings Life and Life eternal?

Travelling all over the world,[11] standing where Martyrs were tortured and killed, we found ourselves walking the Way of the Cross with those who died rather than deny the Faith, crying as we stood where they were tortured, the many priests who died as they had lived - for Mother Church, proclaiming with their sacrifice, loud and clear, they were not dying for a piece of bread. And the haunting question kept coming to us: *Are we in the days of Martyrdom? Will we run from the Way of the Cross like the first Apostles?* Did the Disciples of Jesus recognize Judas in their midst before that dreadful day when he betrayed Our Lord? Did they suspect that he was a thief and a traitor and kept silent? Will we recognize the Judases of today before they lead our Church to Calvary?

We studied Holy Scripture in order to try to get into the Hearts of Jesus and His Mother Mary as they walked to the Cross; we began to dig deeper into their lives; as we did so, we realized the Lord wanted us to show the price both He and His Mother paid for our salvation from her first *yes* at the Annunciation to *His yes* at the Cross. It is no small wonder that the Lord had inspired us to write about this, the life of Jesus and Mary[12] the same year we wrote on the Martyrs.

Attacks on the Church have been coming from new heretics spouting old heresies, and alleged visionaries prophesying the end of the world. Jesus said that no one knows the time and the place except His Heavenly Father. We felt a solemn need to re-emphasize what the Church teaches, that the way to the Kingdom is narrow, and that way is only through Jesus. We hear it said plainly in Holy Scripture that *Jesus is the Way* - the only Way, *the Truth* - the only Truth, *and the Life* - the only Life. The enemy of confusion, Lucifer himself, has been using often unsuspecting instruments to lead the Lord's children astray. The Church does not approve visionaries nor apparitions until they have passed the most intense scrutiny and test of time, *and* shown evidence of fruits of the Holy Spirit. This is important, as we have too long been accused of being a Church of superstition; and nothing could be farther from the truth.

We discovered, through one of our converts working in the Ministry that the existence of *Heaven, Hell and Purgatory* was not being taught in RCIA.[13] Then, the Lord wanting us to understand what He was saying, what should we hear but these teachings of the Church being discredited out of existence, right from the altar, with the Laity not knowing what to believe. We could see that we were in the time of Luther and we were losing our Church and many of us did not know it was happening. In the writing of our twelfth book,[14] we had to do a great deal of research which led us to the writing of the first book of this Trilogy. By the way, you the Laity have proven you do believe and you are not about to let anyone take that reassuring Truth away from you.

St. Teresa of Avila

Martin Luther

We are in another year. We have prayed and prayed, and then we have searched and researched, and always the same thought came: *Find out how it happened and call My children back home.* Now, we believe that this Trilogy is not only for those of you who have left, but has been written to help save Jesus' lambs who are being led to slaughter by Judas goats,[15] right within our Church.

From as far back as 1988, when we began writing about Saint Teresa of Avila,[16] we have had a gnawing, aching desire to write this book. That was when we were first introduced to Martin Luther. St. Teresa and Luther lived in the same century. She obeyed and as a Doctor of the Church[17] is still leading the Faithful to a closer walk with Jesus through His Church. Luther disobeyed and was responsible for the wandering of many innocent lost lambs who followed him. We found ourselves delving deeply into his life, trying to find the answer to the question that gnawed at our hearts: *How could a son, an Ambassador of Christ betray the Church he had taken an oath to obey?*

Each time, we began this Trilogy, it seemed the Lord was calling us to write a different book. We are now firmly convinced this is what the Lord wants us to bring to you, *now!* If the amount of attacks that have been waged during the writing of this book is any indicator that this is the Will of God, we can be fairly certain it is. But then each year, each book was accompanied by blessings and suffering. We cannot explain why. But as always, we wait upon His Will in our lives, praying each day that we are living according to His Will and not ours.

As we have prayed on what the Lord has been doing in our lives, the progression and order of the books we have been writing, and the programs we have been making for EWTN, we discovered the important message the Lord has for all of us - for those within the Church, and those who have left and need to come back. *The Lord is weaving a new garment*, and we are all called to be a part of it. When the Lord comes, who will go with Him and who will stay behind? It has always been up to *Saints, Martyrs and powerful brothers and sisters*, like you, to bring Him and His Church to the world. St. Paul said: *"How then shall they call on Him, in Whom they have not believed? Or how shall they believe Him, of Whom they have not heard? And how shall they hear, without a preacher?"*[18]

Jesus is telling us to be not afraid,[19] reassuring us *"I am the good Shepherd. A good shepherd lays down His life for His sheep."*[20] It is said that no matter how many sheep from different herds are mixed in a field, they will go to their own shepherd, knowing and following his voice. We are Jesus' sheep and He is our Shepherd. He is still preaching to us in His Word, showing us the way, that narrow way to His Father. He is present in His Eucharist to give us strength, that no one may lead us astray.

He has spoken through His Mother. At the many apparitions that have been approved by the Church, and passed the test of time, Our Lord is letting us know that His Mother is still interceding, as she did at Cana and that He is still listening to her, moved by her love for us. Listen to her advice *"Do whatever He tells you."*[21] In one way or another that is basically what our Mother has been saying.

He has always sent us role models when our Church was in trouble, when our world was on the verge of holocaust. Listen and follow the path of these powerful men and women the Lord used to save the Church and the world. Don't buy into poor substitutes that tickle your ears.

He has given us Angels to guide us, to protect us, to aid us for the journey ahead. Don't listen to those who would tell you there are no such spirits as Angels. For if there are no Angels, is there a devil, is there a God? Do you see where they are trying to lead us?

We are in the days where we cannot accept everything we hear, whether by a Priest, a Minister, a President, a teacher, a theologian or a well-meaning friend. So many of our Catholics have been robbed of their Faith, bit by bit; they never realized they were no longer Catholic. The *bad* news is that this slow-moving poison has been fed to us for almost 2000 years; the Good News is we are still here and our Church is still alive, guiding us until the Lord returns.

When we wrote our book *"Scandal of the Cross, and Its Triumph, Heresies throughout the History of the Church,"* we found ourselves warning the Faithful, exposing those *within* the Church who had gone astray and were leading others to do likewise. Now, we embark, at last, to begin a

Journey of Faith which will call those who have left, and arm those who have remained and are under attack. Now, we understand the Lord's purpose in having us wait to write this book. We will endeavor to show you how what came to pass, the 40,000 plus splinters of the One True Cross, was a result of a *few* chipping away at the foundation of the *only* Church dating back to Jesus, the Church which flowed from His pierced Heart on the Cross.

We see now that having us write about the Eucharist, His Mother, His Saints and His Angels, God as the Great Chess Player has been carefully positioning all His pieces in readiness for battle, waging war, correcting the errors that have been circulating about what we as Catholics believe and do not believe. He is placing all of us, the entire Mystical Body of Christ in the front lines preparing for the *Gentle Revolution*, defending our Queen Mother Mary, so that she can, with her Pope and Defenders of the Faith like Mother Angelica, usher in the Age of the Eucharist in the Third Millennium.

We are living in a glorious but challenging time in the Church and in the world. Jesus will be victorious and His victory will light the bright flame of the Holy Spirit and lead our brothers and sisters back home. We believe, the Lord wanted us to reveal to you that what you are hearing within the Church by some who are in error, are old heresies long condemned by the Church centuries ago. Now, with this Trilogy, you will notice that many of these tired old heresies which have been condemned, are what many of the sects that have cropped up in the last 500 years have been espousing and using to attack our young - leading them away from the Truth.

Now, why this book on the Reformation following our book on Martyrs? We believe it is because the Martyrs did not choose to die for a piece of bread, as some of our brothers and sisters insist the Eucharist is. As one of the early Church writers, Tertullian said, *"If the Eucharist is a piece of bread, then we nailed a piece of bread to the Cross."* The Martyrs died for the Lord Who is truly, substantially present in our Church, in His Body, Blood, Soul and Divinity, in His Word and in the faithful who come together to worship Him.

I learned the other day that the true English translation to the word *worship* is *obedience*! And how can you obey Him Whom you do not know, and how can you know Him if you do not attend the Church He founded, the Church with the whole Truth? We believe all our books have been written to make you personally aware of the Treasures we have in our Church, and Whom you leave if you leave the Catholic Church.

In the first book of our Trilogy we have outlined the Treasures that separate us from our non-Catholic brothers and sisters. But they belong to you, too. Jesus wants you to have them. This is an invitation from His vicar Our Pope who has asked us all to evangelize, to our separated family to come Home to the one true Catholic Church, and claim all the Treasures that have been stored for us since Jesus gave them to His Church 2000 years ago.

We want to share the best kept secret in the world, the One Who is alive and desires all His children to be one in Him through the Church He founded, through the Vicar He appointed 2000 years ago to guide us to Him. He is asking you who are reading this Trilogy to come back home, if you have left. He wants to share His Heart with you. He wants to introduce His Mother to you. He is pleading with you who have remained, to learn more about your Faith so that you can teach it to others. We have met some of the strongest Catholics, our converts, those who, upon discovering the One True Church, have come Home.

We believe the Lord is calling *all* His children to come *Home to the Roman Catholic Church* because Jesus wants us all to stand side-by-side, brothers and sisters in Christ, ready to live for her, prepared to die for her, if need be. Is this why He is revealing to you and to them, how and why the breakdown came about? Or does He want you to know how easy it is to lose your Church, all you hold dear?

✟ ✟ ✟

Stay with us; we love you with the Hearts of Jesus and His Mother Mary, the Angels and Saints.

Footnotes

[1]*cf*Jn17:20-23

[2]*This is My Body, This is My Blood, Miracles of the Eucharist* - Book I

[3]Read more about this in Bob and Penny's book: *Heaven, Hell and Purgatory*

[4]Eternal Word Television Network - Mother Angelica, foundress

[5]Penny's baby-sitter would bring her to Bible School while her parents worked.

[6]*Many Faces of Mary, a love story*

[7]Bob and Penny wrote their testimony and their witness in their book: *We came back to Jesus.*

[8]*Scandal of the Cross and Its Triumph, Heresies throughout the History of the Church*

[9]during the Reformation

[10]not only those Catholics who have for whatever reason left Mother Church at this time, but the descendants of those who had been led away from their Church centuries ago.

[11]Doing research for our book and T.V. programs: *Martyrs, They died for Christ.*

[12]*The Rosary, The Life of Jesus and Mary* - Bob & Penny Lord

[13]Rite of Christian Initiation

[14]*Visions of Heaven, Hell and Purgatory* - Bob & Penny Lord

[15]When they want to bring lambs or sheep to market to be sold and slaughtered, they must place a goat into their midst to lead them to the slaughter gate; no sheep or lamb will lead other sheep or lambs to slaughter. And for this reason, this goat is given the name: *Judas Goat.*

[16]in *Saints and other Powerful Women in the Church*

[17]At the present time there are only two women doctors in the Church, but we have a feeling that will not be the case for long.

[18]Rom 10:14

[19]Mt 28:10

[20]Jn 10:11

[21]Jn 2:5

John Wycliff
Birth of the Protestant Reformation

To begin to understand Luther and the division that came about through his instigation, we must go back in history (of the Church) to two priests before him: *John Wycliff* and *Jan Hus*. These men had a phenomenal influence on the forging of Luther's

John Wycliff and his "poor priests"

theology, or rather his attack on the Church. All three of these brilliant men had been ordained to be Christ's *ambassadors*[1] on earth and called to reflect Jesus *in persona Christi Capitas.*[2] This book has been written to enlighten those who are about to be ordained and to remind those already ordained, the reason they were born was to carry the Cross as victim-priest with the Victim-Priest Jesus, as they bring Jesus to the faithful during the ongoing Sacrifice of the Cross - the Mass.

Sometimes I wonder how much greater a mother's labor pains would be, if she could foresee the destruction her soon-to-be-born baby would bring about in the Church, and in the world. Our story takes us to England where the faithful were solid Catholics, fervent about their Catholic Faith and Church. This is the land where the faithful held rosaries in their hands, praying throughout the day. Mrs. Wycliff, did you and your husband pray the rosary with

John and the rest of your children, each night before retiring to bed? [Whenever we interview priests, we most often discover their families prayed the Rosary together, as a family, each night.]

We're in the early 1400's and the cries of a baby are just about to ring out through the streets of Yorkshire. The Wycliff family are anxiously awaiting their newborn child. Little did they know that John Wycliff, the baby that was coming into the world, would one day become a dangerous heretic who would light a spark, and that spark would stoke up old dry wood just waiting to burst into a roaring blaze that would almost consume the Catholic Church in Europe.

Dissent had been brewing in the witches' cauldron. The *Fraticelli,*[3] a small radical sect of the Franciscans, unhappy with the Pope's decision regarding the modification of the Rule of St. Francis, refused to abide by his ruling, claiming he had no authority over them and was extending his power beyond his parameters as Pope. As this fit in with his vendetta against Pope John XII, Louis of Bavaria stepped into the fray, supporting the Fraticelli, purposely adding fuel to the already smoldering fire. Then a friend of Louis, Marsiglio of Padua wrote *Defensor Pacis* where he declared that the state was *superior* to the Church in all matters, with the clear cut purpose of reducing the Pope to a mere figure head. Under this document, the term of the Pope depended on the whims and moods of the Emperor; he could choose and depose the Pope. In other words, *Gallicanism*[4] from the Eighth and Ninth Centuries, long believed dead and buried, had been raising its *decomposed carcass* in the Twelfth, then in the Thirteenth and now in the Fourteenth Century.

The heresies of this, the Fourteenth Century, and the one following, would be responsible for the division and pain that would come about in the Sixteenth Century.

Division had begun in Avignon, France, when the Popes fled from Rome to Avignon and set up the Holy See there for 68 years. After the Papacy returned to Rome a controversy arose, and there was a split, with anti-popes continuing to take up residence in Avignon. This brought about a break with Rome and the chair of Peter, causing the great *Western Schism.*[5] Like a tree whose trunk is damaged with each strike of the loggers ax, so the Church was weakened by this Schism. It was eventually resolved and the Papacy remained in Rome with solely *one Pope*, the true successor of Peter. Councils were called, Bulls were issued, heresies were dispelled but the spirit of anti-papalism once in the air, continued to pollute the Church and its members.

John Wycliff could have been remembered as a *Defender of the Faith*, as the century he was privileged to be born into needed such Saints; instead he is known as a heretic! He came from the gentry, from a family who afforded him the finest education in the best schools. He entered the world-acclaimed Oxford University in around 1345, received his doctorate in theology in about 1372. Considered a philosopher and well thought-of scholar, he continued to be an influence on young minds in Oxford. Believing that God had chosen him to serve Him in the priesthood, he was ordained in 1361.

King Edward III of England had an ongoing feud going with the Papacy over certain papal tributes due the Holy See. Now these had always been traditionally paid by the Crown and Parliament. But in the year 1374, both the King and his court were looking for a way to renege on paying assessments to the Pope. They came up with the bright idea of choosing a cleric to represent the Crown. [The enemy always, beginning with Judas, picks one of Jesus' trusted apostles.] They commissioned Wycliff and, although a priest, he agreed to represent the Monarchy. [So much for separation of Church and State.] Wycliff was to gain much importance and recognition when he wrote several dissertations *disputing* the Pope's claim and upholding the Parliament's right to *limit* the power of the Papacy in the Realm. Was this in obedience to the oath he had taken on the day of his ordination? Was it taken in the light of his sworn loyalty to the Pope or was he influenced by his sworn duty to the Crown?

Next the King sent Wycliff, as *his* emissary, to represent him at a conference in Bruges, Belgium, which was called to settle misunderstandings separating the Papacy and the Crown. Nothing was resolved; the meeting was a failure; but Wycliff gained much prestige. John Gaunt, the King's son, who was well-known for his *anti-papal* sentiments, chose Wycliff to be his clerical advisor. Now to be in the service of John Gaunt, Duke of Lancaster, the son of King Edward III and heir to the throne, was definitely an advantage for someone who had great ambitions and aspirations. Being affiliated with the wealthiest and most influential man in the kingdom, the Duke's friendship would become an invaluable asset when Wycliff was called to stand before the ecclesiastical court to answer charges of heresy.

Now Wycliff had been spouting his own theology in direct opposition to the teachings of the Church for awhile, but the local bishop hesitated to take steps to silence him. As the bold left unchecked only grow bolder, so the day arrived when Wycliff, having gone too far, was called to answer charges of heresy regarding his teachings.

The meeting took place in St. Paul's Church in London, with Wycliff accompanied by the Duke and his formidable entourage. When the bishop went to meet Wycliff and the Duke, there were so many citizens gathered in St. Paul's that the King's marshall had a problem forging a path through the crowd. He began ordering the people to make way for the Duke, pushing and shoving them, when Bishop Courtenay warned the marshall to not exercise any of his magisterial rights within the church. The people stepped to the side and allowed the Duke to make his grand entrance. All went well until the Duke attacked the bishop, hurling threats and ultimatums, using Wycliff's heresy of *Dominion* as his authority. A riot broke out. The Duke, unpopular with the people anyway, found the crowd siding with the bishop. Sadly and predictably the meeting at St. Paul's accomplished nothing. Wycliff was allowed to leave without incident. One of the charges against Wycliff, read at the church, was the very heresy the Duke had tried to use:

Dominion - the right to exercise authority, and indirectly, to hold property, is held from God and is a right that God limits to those in sanctifying grace. Unworthy priests, therefore forfeited this right, and lay lords may deprive them of their benefices.[6] On the other hand, these same lay lords need not fear incurring excommunication in return, since such a censure could only be validly employed solely for a strictly spiritual offense.

Communication lacking, as it was in those days, and unaware the bishops had summoned Wycliff, the Pope issued *five* Bulls against Wycliff, *three* to Bishop Sudbury[7] and Bishop Courtenay, *one* to the King and *one* to Oxford University. He sternly chastised the bishops for not having censured Wycliff; he warned the King that Wycliff's views were not only a threat to the Church but to the state as well; to Oxford University, the Bull decreed they were no longer to allow Wycliff to spout his heresies and they were to hand him over to the Church authorities. The Pope issued a Bull ordering the bishops to investigate Wycliff's 19 propositions (included in his thesis on *Dominion*).

March, 1378, Wycliff presented himself to the bishops' court. Now, the Queen Mother sent her emissary along, bearing a mandate, Wycliff not be punished as a result of the bishops' findings. In deference to her majesty's request, the court ordered Wycliff to cease teaching his heresies and let him go. The Duke intervened as well, invoking the Bishops' Council not to take disciplinary action against Wycliff, and with that *he ordered* Wycliff to cease attacking the Church.

A board of theologians at Oxford ruled that Wycliff's propositions against *Transubstantiation* were heretical and he was to cease teaching them to the school body. The Duke went to his erring friend and cautioned him to obey the University's findings. But Wycliff went too far with his attacks on *Transubstantiation*. When he had challenged the authority of the Papacy, he had some support among the clergy; but disputing the Reality of the True Presence of Jesus in the Holy Eucharist was too much. They could not go along with his heresy, which denied that which the Church has taught down through the ages, that although under the appearance of bread and wine, the consecrated Species are no longer bread and wine but *solely* and completely the Lord in His *Body, Blood, Soul and Divinity*.

Although Wycliff was not known to be *directly* involved with the Peasants' Revolt, inflammatory revolutionary ideas sowed by him and his "poor priests"[8] incited the peasants, bringing about horrendous blood baths, unleashed anger and uncontrolled madness abounding beyond reason. This cost Wycliff most of his sympathizers when they saw the senseless carnage, the veritable horror before their eyes, resulting from his irresponsible rantings and heretical teachings. He lost all credibility at the University and ended his days dying alone and quite unnoticed in 1384. Pope Urban VI, so like our present Pope John Paul II, desiring reconciliation and not the death of a sinner, summoned Wycliff to appear before him. Wycliff refused, claiming he was too ill to attend. The Council of Constance ordered his books burned and his remains removed from consecrated ground as he had died a heretic.

Wycliff's heretical teachings

Wycliff wrote that the Church is a *spiritual* body of the predestined few, and as such cannot have a *physical* head; therefore the Pope was not *Divinely* appointed, and no one was required to obey him. This contradicted Holy Scripture where Jesus said to Peter: *"You are Rock and upon this Rock I will build My Church."* Wycliff's heresy also discounted Pentecost, the birthday of the Church, when the Holy Spirit descended upon the Apostles and they - the *physical church* went out and not only laid hands on the faithful but *taught* them through His Divine Inspiration!

Wycliff went on to say that since the Pope had no *Divine* authority over the Church, then each of the faithful could and should interpret the Bible for himself. And since Wycliff claimed that the Bible was the only true tenet of faith, we can see where this will lead Luther and the many *unsuspecting* lambs who will follow him.

Using the problems and abuses in the hierarchy of the Church of *his* day, Wycliff completely ignored the teaching of the Church that the unworthiness of the Minister does not negate the *sanctity* of the Church and the *sacredness* of the authority passed on to the head of that Church, no matter how unworthy he is to carry out his appointed mission.

Playing God, judge and jury, Wycliff went about remolding the Church's doctrines to his *own* design, a principal teaching being - Human beings are not born with *free will;* some *are pre-destined* by God to eternal damnation, and others are pre-destined by God to be saved.

Satan always induces man to go farther and farther until he is condemned and repents or goes to his death a heretic. Wycliff's attack on the Eucharist in his controversial *De*

Eucharista was the straw that broke the camel's back. He went too far with that one, and lost most of his followers.

Some of his writings which were condemned and yet are proselytized till today are:

(1) he rejected the Papacy;
(2) attacked the hierarchy and the priesthood;
(3) denied the Sacraments;
(4) denied confession;
(5) attacked the Mass;
(6) attacked Transubstantiation;
(7) taking of vows and religious orders in general
(8) endowments left to the Church and in general the wealth of the priests;
(9) what he called the Sale of Indulgences;
(10) he was the precursor of *sola scriptura*
(11) condemned pilgrimages
(12) condemned veneration of Saints

What can we say about Wycliff? A priest put himself and his country before the Kingdom of God and what did he leave behind - open wounds and wandering children seeking the Truth. That which he had begun and that which followed this heretic, for one hundred years after his death, was not a new doctrine but the undermining and weakening of the ancient Doctrines of the Church. And those today who claim they are bringing us new doctrines are just perpetuating what this heretic and all the heretics who preceded him and followed him - attacks against the Church which flowed from Our Lord's open Heart on the Cross.

After you've read the chapter on Martin Luther, come back to the heretical teachings of John Wycliff. Luther admitted to having been influenced by Wycliff and Hus. But if you look at Wycliff's teachings listed above, it's like a manifesto of Luther's attacks. All of the above are part of Luther's 95 questions which were posted on the church door at Wittenberg. Where did he get them? Or did the Protestant Reformation begin with John Wycliff in England and come to its completion through Henry VIII and his followers, again in England? It give us pause to consider.

✝ ✝ ✝

The haunting questions persist, as we try to get into the head and heart of heretics and schismatics who led Catholics away from Mother Church, how can someone turn against the Roman Catholic Church when he knows the Treasures she contains, those necessary for eternal life; how can someone lead others away from our Faith when he knows *Who* is the Head of our Church? It is difficult to comprehend a man betraying the very Church he *knows* was founded by Jesus Himself. We can barely fathom what would possess a priest, bishop or theologian to turn against the Church which he *knows* flowed from Jesus' wounded Heart. How can he go against Jesus, Whom he holds in his hands, Whom he sees come to life because *he*[9] summoned the Holy Spirit down from Heaven upon the gifts he was offering to God the Father on the altar? Our clergy *know* that they were chosen to bring life, the Eucharist - the very Heart of our Church, to the lambs[10] of God. How can they turn away from their Lord Who is *really* present to them and us, Body, Blood, Soul and Divinity, on the Altar, in the Tabernacle, in a Monstrance to be with us, to hear us, to speak to our hearts? How does he live, knowing he is responsible for depriving even one soul from this liberating Sacrament of Salvation? How can he sleep, knowing he is accountable for the innocent losing the everlasting Peace which comes to us in the Sacraments?

"Even those who do not believe that Purgatory exists, by the mercy of God will end up there."[11] We must pray for those who lead our beloved children away from Christ's Church, for He was quite strong when he warned:

"Whoever causes these little ones who believe in me to sin, it would be better for him to have a great millstone hung around his neck and be drowned in the depths of the sea.[12]

As we've travelled through the annals of the Roman Catholic Church,[13] we have sadly discovered that from the very beginning, it has often been those most favored and highly trusted who have betrayed Mother Church: her priests, bishops and theologians. The fact that we are still here, after relentless attacks from within and without, proves beyond a shadow of a doubt that God's only begotten Son founded this Church and hell will not prevail against her, that Jesus is in our Church because He made a promise to be with His children till He comes again.

For 2000 years the battles waged against the Church have been so brutal and devastating, each century was sure the Lord would come in their time and shepherd His flock.

"For the Lord Yahweh says this: I am going to look after My flock Myself and keep it all in view. As a shepherd keeps all his flock in view when he stands up in the middle of his scattered sheep, so shall I keep My sheep in view. I shall rescue them from wherever they have been scattered during the mist and darkness. I shall bring them out of countries where they are; I shall gather them together from foreign countries and bring them back to their own land. I shall pasture them on the mountains of Israel, in the ravines and in every inhabited place in the land. I shall feed them in every good pasturage; the high mountains of Israel will be their grazing ground. There they will rest in good grazing ground; they will browse in rich pastures on the mountains of Israel. I Myself will pasture My sheep, I Myself will show them where to rest - it is the Lord Yahweh Who speaks. I shall look for the lost one, bring

back the stray, bandage the wounded and make the weak strong. *I shall watch over the fat and the healthy. I shall be a true shepherd to them.* "[14]

This was the promise made again by Jesus when He promised He would not leave us orphans; He would be with us till the end of the world; he would not let hell prevail against His Church. This is our hope when we are discouraged and feel helpless, Jesus in His Word speaks to us, reassuring us; Jesus in the Eucharist strengthens us for our Way to the Cross. For if we are truly to follow Jesus, it must be through the Way of the Cross. There are no shortcuts, as the enemy would have you believe. The only shortcuts are to hell.

And to those who have strayed, the Lord warns:

As for you My sheep, the Lord Yahweh says this: I will judge between sheep and sheep, between rams and he-goats. Not content to graze in good pasture, you trample down the rest; not content to drink clear water, you muddy the rest with your feet. And My sheep must graze on what your feet have trampled, drink what your feet have muddied. Very well then, the Lord Yahweh says this: I myself am now about to judge between fat sheep and lean sheep. Since you have butted all the lean sheep with your rump and shoulders and horns, until you have chased them away, I am going to come and rescue My sheep from being cheated; I will judge between sheep and sheep.[15]

Yahweh, God the Father sent His only Son to lead us to graze in green pastures - the Church Jesus founded, to be filled with clear water - the water of Baptism, one of the Sacraments Jesus left to us. He continues to warn those who lead us astray to repent and come back to Him. He in His Word gives hope to us and to those who have been led away from His fold. God's message is: We need not graze in pastures trampled down by heretics and schismatics, or drink water that has been muddied by the enemy. We pray that this Trilogy opens your heart and mind to what Our Lord is saying to you, for this time, for this Church, for the world.

The ongoing war to destroy the Church

It started in the Garden of Eden when Satan told Eve a lie and she and Adam lost eternal joy and life with the Father. And he has been telling lies ever since; God trying to help His children, and Lucifer fighting Him every inch of the way, taking as many to hell as he can. The sad news is that the instruments, down through the history of the Church, have been men and women of God. How the devil rejoices when he can flaunt one of these fallen ones victoriously before God.

Beginning with the First Century, till today, the Church has had to face one heretical and schismatic attack after another (attack). Satan did not wait for one heresy to be defeated before he instigated another, and always using those who *claimed to know more* than our first Pope and his successors. But God has always raised up powerful men and women to fight the Church's battles, putting on the Armor of God, correcting the errors that their fellow theologians, priests and bishops had extolled.

Why is it important that you read *Scandal of the Cross and Its Triumph, Heresies throughout the History of the Church* as a companion to this Trilogy? Because you will discover the root problems that began in the Church, and have cropped up over and over again down through the ages, are firmly entrenched in the teachings of the Heretics and Schismatics in this book and the Cultists in Trilogy Book III.[16] You need to know! Our Church is being bitterly threatened by enemies within and those without, Satan pulling out all stops, full steam ahead. We know that other generations before us felt the same way, but all the signs point to a great holocaust, if we do not stand up and take back our Church.

There is only one way this can happen. You must become informed. You must get involved. It's your Church. Jesus has commanded you through our Popes by the merits of your Baptism into the Catholic Church to defend and protect our Church. *Jesus needs you! Your Church needs you!*

Footnotes

[1]one of the titles given a priest

[2]in the person of Christ the Head of the Church

[3]condemned by Pope John XII in the bull *Sancta Romana*

[4]Read more about this in the chapter on the Battles.

[5]For more on Avignon, read Bob & Penny Lord's book, *This Is My Body, This Is My Blood, Miracles of the Eucharist Book I*

[6] A *benefice* historically has been a grant of land for life, in reward for services rendered. In the Church it came to mean an ecclesiastical office which carried certain obligations, as well as being a source of income for the office-holder. - New Catholic Encyclopedia

[7]He was the local ordinary who had hesitated calling Wycliff in, hoping he would cease his attacks on Catholic Doctrine.

[8]many of whom were not priests at all, simply Wycliff's puppets

[9]through the Holy Orders he received on the day of his ordination

[10]Catholics

[11]*Heaven, Hell and Purgatory* by Bob and Penny Lord

[12]Mk 9:42-47 - Is Jesus referring to *"little ones"* as those who become like little children having the vulnerable open trust and faith of little children, those innocent souls who through another, with no fault of their own, have their faith weakened or suffer a loss of Faith?

[13]For more on the heresies that have attacked the Church for 2000 years, read Bob & Penny's book: *Scandal of the Cross and Its Triumph, Heresies throughout the History of the Church.*

[14]Ez 34:11-17

[15]Ez 34:17-22

[16]*Cults, Battle of the Angels*

Jan Hus

Hero or Heretic?

Who was the real Jan Hus? Born into controversy, controversy would follow him all his life and long after he was laid to rest. There is still much argument - some remembering him fondly as a reformer, a hero, and martyr; others as a dissident, an agitator and heretic. The hurts and divided loyalties resulting from *this* one wrong turn in the road by a priest who meant well, would breed disharmony and disunity that would remain unresolved among the Czech people, in one way or the other, till today. There was a devastating

Woodcarving of the Death of Jan Hus

aftermath to his disobedience; it sparked the flame of revolution, the results of which would bring about a splitting of the Church and the world of his time and place; it would ultimately become a dangerous weapon in the hands of Martin Luther which would propel the next century into chaos. If Jan Hus had lived to see how his actions would be played out on the world stage, would he had persisted in his disobedience? *Was it worth it?*

How did it happen? When we wrote of the heretics and heresies of the past,[1] we cried, as we journeyed through the lives of men who had loved the Church and had gone astray; pride coupled with stubbornness leading them far from their first love - Mother Church, many never to return. Not trusting that God would act through obedience, and judging they were right, they had refused to obey. We often talk of the dead bodies left behind by a much loved priest or bishop who leaves the Church for whatever reason, or falls into heresy, separating from the authority of the Church. We always talk about his/her followers. What happened to them? This is the story of one such ambassador of Christ, and once again we find ourselves grieving, tears welling up in our eyes - for the loss of a brother, for those thousands who followed him into heresy, and most importantly for our Lord Jesus and Mother Church.

Will the real Jan Hus stand up?

Jan Hus was born in Bohemia[2] in 1369. Born in turbulent times, his whole life would be one of turbulence. He was highly educated, having received a B.A. in 1393, and a M.A. in 1396 in Prague. He was ordained in 1400, and was assigned to the Chapel of Bethlehem - *House of Bread*;[3] so it would appear the Lord had placed His ambassador in a very symbolic place to begin his life, as a vessel through whom the Lord would bring the *Bread of Life* to His people.

However, God's plan is never the enemy's plan. The Bethlehem Chapel and the university had become a hotbed of radicals and reformers who had been incited by an earlier version of Hus, Jan Milíc, a priest who left his post and preached reform all over Prague. *He* was the forerunner of Jan Hus. Hus was influenced by him and his teachings. Hus received a bachelor's degree in theology in 1404, enabling him to teach philosophy and theology at the university and preach at the Bethlehem Chapel. What an awesome privilege to mold young minds and form future priests, but what a terrifying responsibility!

We know that he was blessed with much schooling. Had education become the Master and not the servant of God? Was he getting so much *head* knowledge, his *heart* knowledge was suffering, and along with the heart, the Church? Had he lost that *synthesis*, that great need for the intermingling of heart and head knowledge, without which we cannot truly serve the Lord? Did the enemy of God tell him that when he believes he is right, he is above the authority of the Church and did not have to obey? Was he above the Church's wisdom that prohibits us from reading heretical literature, out of fear we would be confused and fall into error? Did he suffer from the sin of pride in believing that he could play with fire and not get burned? Now Hus was aware of all the heresies that preceded him and his time. How did he allow himself to flirt with the teachings of John Wycliff, knowing they had been condemned?

As time stands still for no one, neither do the influences that color our lives. He became fascinated with John Wycliff's treatises; He wanted more. Actually, he became the prime follower and proclaimer of Wycliff's condemned teachings. He joined Jerome of Prague, another Czech reformer, who had actually began studying and teaching on the Wycliff errors before Hus.

We're not sure who was outdoing whom, Hus or Jerome of Prague, but between the two, they were enlarging and spreading the Wycliff doctrine all over Prague, Hus began speaking out more and more radically, leveling accusations at the Church in the form of reform. Now revolutionaries like Jerome had been making the faithful aware of the abuses, the avarice and self-interest which had infected the episcopacy, the simony being practiced by many bishops. But it had been mere mumbling, with the mumbling turning into rumbling, and then through Hus the rumbling erupting into a fierce roar. Did *Father* Jan Hus, a priest, have license to air these indictments, maligning the apostles he had sworn to obey, and was it worth the irreparable division and dissension that came about?

Jan Hus and Jerome of Prague not only adopted Wycliff's theology, they expanded it. They:

1. Denied the Primacy of the Popes
by violently attacking bishops, priest, friars and religious of all natures. Remember, Jan Hus was an ordained priest.

2. Denied all the Sacraments

3. Denied Transubstantiation - but insisted that the Faithful receive the Eucharist under both Species. *That doesn't make sense!*

4. Denied Purgatory

5. Denied Confession to a Priest

6. Condemned veneration of relics

7. Condemned what they considered the sale of Indulgences.

8. Advocated individual interpretation of the Bible

9. Faith alone, not good works were the means of salvation.[4]

10. Advocated Predestination - man had no free will

"He did not speak with the wisdom of the Apostles, but with the frenzy of a sectary."[5,6] And so, instead of bringing about reform, it gave leaven to a revolution. He was a rabble-rouser. Hus made enemies! But not with the average Czech; they followed him blindly. Possibly his greatest downfall was that he was so accepted by the common man. They clung to his every word. Did that cause the sinister dragon of pride to build up in him? Was he caught up in the adulation so much, he threw caution to the wind? Was the notoriety he began to receive enough to take away any fear of reprisal from the state or the Church?

He drew *many* to his preaching, his passionate call to moral reform - the much needed word they were hungry to hear. There was so much injustice, the few with so much and the many with little or nothing. They needed him and his word of hope for a new world. He spoke with a passion that appealed to their spirit. He cared and they knew it. It was obvious to them, he loved them, he loved Jesus and he loved the Church. People came from far and wide to hear him. They loved him! He became a national hero. But the more he got involved, interpreting Holy Scripture (according to Wycliff's writings), the more he wrote one controversial thesis after the other concerning the Word, and spiritual life. With each passing day, and each added incendiary sermon, he was treading more and more on dangerous ground. But with each heretical speech, he was also winning the people over. *What to do?*

Priest, Rector, Hero or Heretic?

His bold and unrelenting denunciation of the episcopacy, resulted *first* in his getting denounced in Rome in 1407. And then the following year, in 1408, he was banned from preaching by the Archbishop of Prague - Sbinko von Hasenburg who had received this directive straight from Pope Innocent VII. As we have often said, if there is not enough trouble brewing inside the Church, threatening to spill over, all we need is the state to get involved! And involved they did! King Wenceslaus IV, having an ax to grind, ousted the Germans[7] who were running the University of Prague and appointed *guess who* as rector? You guessed right - Jan Hus!

What did Hus do? Upon stepping into his new role and responsibility, a ready-made audience of fresh young minds at his disposal, Hus launched a campaign introducing *Wycliff's doctrines* into this most powerful group of future priests! Now, knowing the influence these teachings would have, knowing he was not only leading *them* into heresy - he was causing the whole Church in Bohemia to plunge into error, he nevertheless stuck to his guns, and forged straight ahead. The Archbishop of Prague issued a Bull ordering all material containing Wycliff's writings destroyed!

This was followed by Hus being excommunicated in 1410 and again in 1412. False gods are always ready to betray you and, like rats on a sinking ship, predictably desert you in time of need. And so, knowing he had gone too far, and desiring to close the rift he had caused with the Church, King Wenceslaus had Hus removed as rector of the University. Hus knew he was in trouble; the King had shattered his last hope; he appealed to the aristocracy and they offered him asylum. Under the protection of the nobility, Hus wrote his most important work: *De Ecclesiae*, against the Church. Rather than risk his followers suffering the pains of an interdict,[8] as a result of his excommunication, Hus left Prague.

The Council of Constance (1414-1417) was summoned by the bishops. Emperor Sigismund of The Holy Roman Empire of Germany assured Hus he would have safe-conduct to the Council. With that security in hand, Hus finally agreed to submit himself and his writings to the judgment of the Church, by appearing before the general Council called by the bishops. As the Pope was struggling with many problems in the Vatican, he absented himself from the proceedings. Hus set out to appear before the Council. Now the Emperor had, *to say the least*, used poor judgment granting Jan Hus a guarantee of safe-conduct, as he had no jurisdiction in the ecclesiastical court. So while he could guarantee that Jan Hus would arrive safely at the Council, he had no control over what would happen at the Council.

What sadly faced Hus and his companion, Jerome of Prague, when they arrived in Constance were Dominicans who threw them into prison. After due deliberation, thirty propositions from his work were denounced and condemned! Hus and Jerome were given an opportunity to recant their doctrines *(and those of Wycliff)* and they refused.

Sin not contained spreads. When we threaten the state, it does not have the loving compassion of Our Lord and His Church. When Hus' disobedience to the Church became a threat to the state, he was condemned, not only for his writings and heretical preaching, but for the civil disorder and insurrection his sermons incited. For this, Hus was sentenced to death and burned at the stake on July 6, 1415.

His followers immediately declared him a martyr! He became a national symbol of Bohemia, a cause for the young to fight! His death enraged them. There was fighting in the streets. Hus' death ignited a fire which would not be extinguished for almost twenty years, his Czech followers who were young - having been largely influenced by him in the University, fighting Catholic Germans[9] sympathetic and loyal to the Church. This bloody warfare in Bohemia and Moravia would last for almost twenty years, from 1419-1436, brother killing brother, the radical nationalist Bohemian party consisting of Czechs, fighting the conservative Catholic party comprised mainly of Germans. What started as a religious war soon turned into a war of nationalities, one side dealing retribution upon the other, brutally and without conscience and all in the Name of Jesus and fatherland.

The Council of Basel (1431-1449) offered the Hussites[10] a means of returning to the Church with the *Compactata of Prague.* Now within the Hussites, there were two factions: the Ultraquists and the Taborites. The Ultraquists accepted the Council's offer and the Taborites rejected the olive branch of peace from Mother Church. The fighting resumed, even more violently than before. [Jesus' prophecy that daughter would go against mother, mother against daughter, son against father and father against son....has been perpetuated from His death on the Cross till today.][11] The Ultraquists were defeated in the battle of Lipan in 1434 and two years later Sigismund (who was largely responsible for Hus' death, having unwittingly led him to his death) ascended to the throne of Bohemia. When the Council of Basel met with the Hussites, after conferring together, it was agreed to the satisfaction of both that:

(1)the Word of God was to be preached freely, but only by those who had received their mission from the Church;

(2)the use of the Chalice was conceded to the laity i.e. Communion under the Species of wine was conceded, provided it was believed and taught that Christ was wholly present under either of the Species;

(3)mortal sins, particularly those causing public scandal, were to be punished in conformity with Divine and ecclesiastical laws, though only by legitimate authority;

(4)the Church had the right of ownership and so did the clergy, but they were obliged to use their goods in an entirely just way.

With this, the Hussite movement died out; the wars ended; but the effects live on till today - Lutheranism the religion of former Hussites and Catholicism of those who remained faithful to the Church. *But did the Hussite war end?* To the foolish yes, but did it not continue through Luther and the Thirty Years War, one after the other? Did it not spread throughout Europe through the disobedience of King Henry?[12] *"The evil that man does lives long after him,"* is a truth that many have forgotten and those alive are obliged to remember.

When Wycliff weaved his web of disobedience to the Vicar of Christ on earth, he spun the abolishment of Church Dogma and belief in the Sacraments, as well. And just as when the spider's web is not swept away, it spreads, so this

Woodcarving of Martin Luther and Jan Hus revealing their relationship

heresy was resurrected, supported and promoted by *Jan Hus*. The errors promulgated by these priests were condemned and they were excommunicated, but the scars remain. Wycliff died in his bed; Hus was burned at the stake.

As we do not go to Heaven without help, so we do not fall into the depths of hell alone. We can hear the heresies of these two priests resurfacing years later, when Luther resounds and re-echoes the same errors. Luther said on many occasions that he had been influenced by the writings of Wycliff and Hus. Did he not know that these heresies had been condemned by the Council of Constance in 1417, and that the *primacy* of the Pope was confirmed for all time in the Ecumenical Council of Florence in 1443? Did Luther put himself above this authority (the Pope) commissioned by Jesus, and the traditional teachings of the Church? Jesus said He would send down the Holy Spirit; and that Spirit has been Divinely inspiring and instructing our Popes ever since, with the *enemy* attacking that authority in one way or the other.

Hus forgave his executioners, called upon the Name of Jesus and died reciting the Creed. *How did it happen Jan Hus?* Instead of the destruction you were responsible for initiating, I prefer to remember you by your last words:

We believe in one God,
the Father, the Almighty,
maker of heaven and earth,
of all that is seen and unseen.
We believe in one Lord, Jesus Christ,
the only Son of God,
eternally begotten of the Father
God from God, Light from Light
true God from true God,
begotten, not made, one in Being with the Father.
Through Him all things were made.
For us men and for our salvation
He came down from heaven:
by the power of the Holy Spirit
    He was born of the Virgin Mary, and
       became Man.
For our sake He was crucified under Pontius
Pilate;
He suffered, died and was buried.
On the third day he rose again
    in fulfillment of the Scriptures;
He ascended into Heaven
and is seated at the right hand of the Father.
He will come again in glory to judge the
    living and the dead,
and His kingdom will have no end.
We believe in the Holy Spirit, the Lord,
    the giver of life,
Who proceeds from the Father and the Son.
With the Father and the Son He is worshiped
    and glorified.
He has spoken through the Prophets.
We believe in one holy Catholic and apostolic
Church.

We acknowledge one baptism for the
forgiveness of sins.
We look for the Resurrection of the dead,
and the life of the world to come. Amen.

Footnotes

[1]*Scandal of the Cross and Its Triumph, Heresies throughout the History of the Church*

[2] Czech nation

[3]translation for Bethlehem

[4]Did Martin Luther get this from Jan Hus? Luther admitted being extremely influenced by the teachings of Jan Hus.

[5]*sectary*-member of a sect, a dissident of an established church

[6]*cf*Emile de Bonnechose, a Protestant admirer

[7]they were citizens of Bohemia who favored the Church

[8]An *interdict* is a censure that deprives the faithful, either lay or cleric, of certain spiritual benefits but permits them to remain in communion with the Church. A local interdict does not forbid the administration of the Sacraments to the dying if regulations are observed, but it does forbid, with several exceptions, the celebration of any Divine services in the territory. (If you would like to read more on this, read *The Catholic Encyclopedia* - Broderick, from which we retrieved this information.)

[9]who had been citizens of Bohemia for centuries

[10]followers of Jan Hus

[11]Mt 10:35

[12]Read about Luther, Henry and the Wars fought in the following chapters.

Martin Luther

Reformer or Revolutionary?

Martin Luther

Having grown up in a home and a family where all religions were respected, we have always had a sincere love for our Protestant and Jewish brothers and sisters.

When our grandson Rob wanted to attend a university near home which was Lutheran, we felt no real threat to his faith walk as a Catholic. From the time he was a little boy, he had been steeped in his Faith. In the beginning Rob was planning to stay at the Lutheran University for one year, and then go on to a Catholic school not close to home. He was surrounded by such love and fellowship at that university, he stayed on to graduate from there. His roommates, mostly Lutherans, are still among his best friends, one of whom we call grandson and he calls us Grandma and Grandpa. We maintain to this day that some of the nicest people are in that school. This book and this chapter is written with much love and fond memories of them.

Our minds and hearts transport us to the day we walked toward the Admissions office of the Lutheran University Rob was planning to enter. I had little or no trepidation, as

I remembered the monthly ecumenical meetings our pastor Monsignor Tom O'Connell had with the ministers and rabbi in our community, and the spirit-filled Thanksgiving service we *all,* Catholics, Protestants and Jews, attended together at our church. I guess I was fondly reminiscing over the time Monsignor invited the local Lutheran Minister and his congregation to attend our Sunday Mass. When Mass was over Monsignor invited his guests to remain. They took him up on his invitation and then asked questions about the Mass and about our differences. The one thing I remember vividly was the pastor saying, *"We grieve until we are all united, once again, under the one Chair of Peter."* This chapter is also for you, Pastor. And this book is for our shared dream.

On this particular sunny California day, we were greeted *warmly* by a young man from the admissions office. Everything was going fine. He assured us that 40% of the student body was Catholic, and that there was not, and never would be, any attempt to influence Rob or any of the other Catholic students to leave their Catholic Faith. I guess, I was feeling pretty good. I confidently responded, *"Well, with the dialogue between the Pope and the Lutheran churches, it looks as if the day will not be far off, that we will be one."* The young man shocked us with his response: *"After Pope John Paul II's most recent statement about Confession, I am afraid we have been set back 400 years."* The Pope's *"recent* statement" was only a continuation of the mandate given by Jesus to His first Pope and Bishops, the Apostles:

"I assure you, whatever you declare bound on earth shall be bound in Heaven, and whatever you declare loosed on earth shall be loosed in Heaven."[1]

Although it seems incredulous that we would suddenly be struck dumb, we were! A gentle and very kind voice, but very firm, that of our grandson, came forth: *"I don't know about you, but I need to hear that my sins are forgiven.''* The young man smiled and replied: *"We knew, from the letters of recommendation, Rob, that you would be an asset to our university; now we know you will be a leader! Welcome to our school.''* This chapter is also for that young man.

This chapter is also for the professor who insisted that Rob be allowed to present his *Catholic* belief as to what St. Paul was saying, when some over zealous Fundamentalists wanted to silence him. And lastly, this is for the most precious grandson in the world, as we recall his words: *"It really hurts when I see the division that came about because Luther chose to work outside of the church, rather than inside.''*

From what we've written above, it's pretty obvious that we have many Protestant friends, and of those, most are Lutherans. So this chapter is by no means meant to demean the Lutheran brothers and sisters, or any of our Protestant brothers and sisters. We're told that many of the Protestants of today don't follow the teachings of their fathers-in-faith, i.e., Luther, Calvin and etc. But these fathers-in-faith are the main causes for the break which separated us from the Church founded by Jesus. We have to tell the story of what happened more for our Catholic brothers and sisters, but also for any of our separated brethren who have also asked the question "Why?" We pray that the account we give of what happened is objective. We will be telling it from the Catholic viewpoint, but our goal is to just to inform, not to judge. We, too, wait for the day when all may be one as Jesus prayed at the Last Supper.[2] We love you.

✝ ✝ ✝

Luther's act of disobedience opened the door to others disobeying him and then others disobeying them and on and on, until it all began to fall apart. In his own lifetime, Luther was to see those who originally followed him, leaving because they disagreed with one or other of his rules. Luther lamented over this toward the end of his life, as he prepared to face the Father. He said, he had tried to get rid of *one* Pope and he created *one hundred* popes.

The fragmentation that was to deluge the Church began with one act of *disobedience.* It is difficult for us to believe that Luther knew what the ramifications of his one act of disobedience would be, and how far-reaching the devastation would be. But as with all of us, once we're on a road of destruction more than reconstruction, it is so *hard* to turn back. One word leads to another, one wound is not allowed to heal before another is inflicted. Anger, one of Satan's invaluable tools of division leads to more anger and then all paths to reconciliation are blocked. For some reason, it is easier to say something wounding than to say *"I am sorry."* We know, the only difference between Judas' betrayal and that of Peter, was Peter said over and over again: *"Forgive me, Lord, I am a sinner."*

Luther Fact or Fiction? *Reformer or Revolutionary?*

"It was from our ranks that they took their leave not that they really belonged to us; for if they belonged to us, they would have stayed with us. It only served to show that none of them was ours."[3]

Martin Luther was born in Eisleben, Germany, November 10, 1483, into a very strict, stern family. There was no room for affection in this family which put discipline and work ahead of love. Hard times struck the family when the father was accused of having killed another farmer in a fit of temper. It is told till today in the village of Morha, how he fled in the middle of the night, his wife heavy with child. One time, his father, in a wild rage, beat him so mercilessly, Luther ran away from home. He never crossed his father again, but never forgave him, either. When he committed what he termed a small infraction *"because of a worthless little nut,"* his very stoic, unbending mother, in an effort to break his strong will, flogged and flogged him until he bled, unmoved by his pleading, he would be good. Into this type of family and environment Martin Luther was to pick up his tendency to flare wildly at a drop of the hat, if someone dared contradict or question him. This was the lesson he learned from his parents. It worked for them; why not him?

He claimed he received the same harsh treatment from his teachers, being whipped as many as 15 times a day, out of no fault of his own. Was this (and we make no excuse for the abuse of anyone, no less a child) as a result of his bullheaded stubbornness and unwillingness to conform and take direction? Instead of accomplishing the desired effect, did they share with his parents the responsibility for the final end product Luther became? Protestant writers say he had a "violent, despotic, uncontrolled nature" - *"his will and his alone, they declare, he dogmatically set up as the only standard he wished to be recognized, followed and obeyed."*[4]

Like many other poor children, he would sing in the streets, begging for money. A very kind wealthy woman, Ursula Cotta, took pity on him and brought him into her home, where things looked up for him. He learned the finer things in life; his roughness was softened by the association of the fine people who visited his benefactress. Due to her benevolence, he was educated in the finest Catholic schools, and then went on to a highly respected Catholic University, where at age *twenty* he received a Master´s Degree of *Philosophy*. His focus was to become a lawyer,[5] and then without notice to the amazement and displeasure of his father, he suddenly shifted his direction and entered the Augustinian Monastery on July 17, 1505, after which in 1507 he was ordained a Catholic priest.

Martin Luther as a monk

Why did Luther enter the Augustinians and become a priest? He told varying stories. To some he said it was because of his harsh treatment at home. To others, it was because he saw his friend die as the result of being struck by lightning. Frightened, he had begged St. Anna, *"Save me and I will enter the Augustinians as a monk."* He also said that the reason he entered was because he was so despondent and wanted to spend his lifetime in contemplation. The sins, real and imagined that he had committed, weighed so heavily on him, he said he was afraid God would strike him down if he did not become a monk.

When he offered his first Mass, he felt so unworthy he was tormented and full of fear, so much so he would have bolted from the altar had not his Prior stopped him. He was afraid God would smite him. Was this the reason, later on, for his unrelenting drive to do away with the Mass: If he was not worthy, then no one was, and then should no one celebrate the Holy Mass?

Luther and Rome

Much is said about the reason Luther came out against the Church. Although many writers have used his visit to Rome as a major contributing factor to Luther's rebellion against what he termed a decadent church, Luther's time in Rome in no way shook his convictions about the Church or her vicar.

"His faith in the Church and in its system was not at that time seriously affected."[6]

Luther *"returned from Rome as strong in his faith as when he left to visit it. In a certain sense his sojourn in Rome **strengthened**[7] his religious convictions."*[8] For a good six years *after* his return from Rome, he lectured, preached and wrote on the *Treasures* of the Catholic Faith and its outpourings of Grace such as: the *Mass, Indulgences*,[9] and *prayer* according to the *traditional teachings* of the Church.

To those who write of his disaffection with the Papacy, let us quote from Luther himself, and what he wrote *shortly after* his momentous visit to Rome.[10]

"If Christ had not entrusted all power to a man (the Pope), *the Church would not have been perfect because there would have been no order, and each one would have been able to say he was led by the Holy Spirit. This is what the heretics did, each one setting up his own principle. In this way as many Churches arose as there were heads. Christ therefore wills, in order that all may be assembled in one unity, that His power be exercised by one man to whom also He commits it. He has, however, made this Power so strong that He has loosed all the powers of Hell, without injury, against it. He says: 'The gates of Hell shall not prevail against it,' as though He said: 'They will fight against it but never overcome it,' so that in this way it is made manifest that this power is in reality from God and not from man. Wherefore whoever breaks away from this unity and order of the Power, let him not boast of enlightenment and wonderful works, as our Picards and other heretics do, for much better is obedience than the victims of fools, who know not what evil they might do.'"*

Now we ask you, does that sound like the man who

Pope Leo X

was troubled by what he saw in Rome? And if he was so disillusioned with Rome, why did he write this, almost *six years before* he posted his attacks on what he called *"decadent Rome?"* But, if you read his words, written shortly after his return from Rome, in the context of what *resulted* from his much later denunciation of the Church, you want to cry. He actually sounds like a defender of the Church who was fighting the injustices he later espoused. We concede, there is rarely a revolution without a cause. But revolutions settle nothing; they merely replace one wrong with another. It is said that when Luther began his offensive against the Church, it was basically to address some problems within the Church, like the selling of Indulgences.

Now let us address this matter of Indulgences. In 1514, Pope Leo X had granted an Indulgence to those donating money toward the building of a new Basilica in Rome - St. Peter's. Although his Bull required *the usual conditions* of penance and contrition, it became highly controversial. Some say, this was the impetus behind Luther posting his 95 theses against *Papal Authority, Indulgences, and Faith and Good Works* to the door of the church in Wittenburg[11] in 1517. But this was a good *three years* after Pope Leo X granted the Indulgence! Why did Luther wait *ten years* to come out against Rome and the Holy See, and *three years* to come out against Indulgences?

Historians have written that when he had visited Rome, he derived his information on what was happening in the

Vatican from a Roman *guide*. Oh my Lord; this is what he based his attack on the Church that he vowed to love and obey! Let's talk about guides! We have been using guides in Rome for almost twenty years. Guides of every nation teach what the government dictates, and if you want to know about

Luther nailed his 95 theses to the door of the University at Wittenburg

Pagan Rome, or Pagan Paris, or Pagan anywhere, for that matter, you have no problem; ask the guide. But if you want to know about the Church, very few guides are authentically Catholic, no less Christian. He not only wrote extensively about the depravity he discovered in Rome[12] in his book *Table Talk,*[13] he also admitted that he celebrated Mass maybe *once* or at the most *ten* times when he was there. What happened? What was his priority? It certainly does not sound like it was the Mass and his priesthood!

What were Luther's 95 theses?

Indulgences

As far back as 1515, Luther was becoming more and more controversial, with theories swiftly, dangerously snow-balling, plumetting downward, accelerating wildly toward serious error. He was already being called a heretic![14] He became more and more unpopular. As his views, contrary to Catholicism, escalated, so did his bad name. He arrogantly challenged anyone and everyone who would dare to defend the Church against his theoretically unsound, completely unfounded doctrinal attacks on the Faith, to a debate.

He wandered farther and farther from his priestly duties and started to publicly question sacred beliefs of the Church. His attacks grew bolder and bolder, unchecked and undisciplined, until Luther attacked the Pope. He used a Bull written by Pope Leo X, granting an Indulgence to anyone donating to the building of St. Peter's Basilica, to come out viciously against the Church. Now, all his accusations were unfounded. Pope Leo X had granted a most simple and wholly acceptable Indulgence, according to Church law. [But then, Luther wanted *all law* abolished, that which is found in the Old *and* New Testaments.)

Luther knew that the Pope had met all the conditions necessary to grant an Indulgence, whether *plenary*[15] or *partial.*[16] Luther knew, as do all priests, *that an Indulgence can only remit the punishment due for serious sins* after a penitent has received absolution *of those sins through the Sacrament of Penance.* He knew that *one must be baptized, a member of the Church who has not been excommunicated, in a state of Grace; and have a genuine sorrow for the sins committed, with a firm resolve to not sin again.*

Luther knew, when he posted those 95 theses with Indulgences as the main target, that the Church teaches:

"An Indulgence is obtained through the Church who, by virtue of the power of binding and loosing[17] granted her by Jesus Christ, intervenes in favor of individual Christians and opens for them the treasury of the merits of Christ and the Saints to obtain from the Father of mercies the remission of the temporal punishments due for their sins. Thus the Church does not want to simply come to the aid of these Christians, but also to spur them to works of devotion, penance, and charity.[18]

Luther knew that the granting of an Indulgence has never had anything to do with the forgiveness of sins, and it does not grant anyone a license to go out and sin again, as

Luther and many who have followed have erroneously alleged. Luther accused the Church of using Indulgences for material gain, forgiving a person all his sins in return for sums of money donated to the Pope, a bishop or a priest; in essence the penitent would pay his way to Heaven, free of all sins, without remorse for his sins or intention to change his life. *Ridiculous!* That would mean that the Church was not only contradicting herself and all she has taught for 2000 years, she was contradicting Jesus Who commissioned His future Apostles to *forgive sins* in the Name of the Father, and of the Son and of the Holy Spirit, Amen. Luther knew that the *Church* as His Body *never* goes against *Christ* the Head, and that as Head of the Church Jesus assigned the forgiveness of sins to be administered *solely* by our priests through the Sacrament of Penance! Yet, he blasphemed against Mother Church, accusing her falsely.

Today, enlightened non-Catholics can see the sad misunderstanding and deception that spread throughout Europe, maligning a holy Pope who had full authority to not only grant and proclaim Indulgences, but also to dispense these spiritual favors in order to encourage and reward charitable contributions, and to allocate, if he so pleases, these donations to a church - as Pope Leo X did for the erection of St. Peter's Basilica. It is not for us to say, but we can wonder: Did Luther begin a revolution and justify his disobedience based on a false accusation? We pray he knew no better, but his education seems to contest that premise. However we leave it, as with all things, up to God.

He not only said that the granting of an Indulgence had no value in God's Eyes, Luther claimed that after the gaining of an Indulgence, the penitent was thrust into a state of immortal sin - even after having received absolution of his sins! I guess he was saying that an Indulgence wiped out the Sacrament of Penance. And yet, the Lord said: *"Truly I* say to you, whatever you bind on earth shall be bound in Heaven and whatever you loose on earth shall be loosed in Heaven." We lost 6,000,000 innocent lambs because they believed him and accepted his false teachings.

Luther said in his theses: "*Christians should be taught that he who gives to the poor, or assists the needy, does better than he who purchases Indulgences.*"[19] I couldn't help thinking, this sounds suspiciously like what Judas protested when Mary Magdalen anointed Jesus' Feet with expensive oil: "*Why was not this perfume sold? It could have brought three hundred silver pieces and the money have been given to the poor.*"[20] Luther, knowing that Indulgences, used especially to relieve or release Poor Souls from suffering in Purgatory has infinite value in God's eyes,[21] did all he could to block people from seeking Indulgences or for that matter praying for the Poor Souls in Purgatory, claiming there was no such place, although from the time of the Old Testament, we have believed in Purgatory.

Looking back, Luther said that he had not known what an Indulgence was. Now, for a Doctor of Theology and Professor to post 95 theses dealing primarily with something he knew nothing about sounds farcical; we would laugh except the consequences were so far-reaching and disastrous, we instead cry. Especially when you consider that prior to his posting these theses, he had preached countless homilies in favor of the Church's teachings on *Indulgences*. His attack on Indulgences were not done out of ignorance, but out of a larger design - to weaken and eventually destroy the Papacy and the Church. Judas received thirty pieces of silver. Luther, and I use *his* words, jeopardized his soul, suffering excommunication for what?

"*I am at Wittenburg. I, Doctor Martin Luther, make it known to all inquisitors of the faith, bullies, and rocksplitters, that I enjoy here abundant hospitality, an open house, a well-*

supplied table, and marked attention; thanks to the liberality of our duke and prince, the Elector of Saxony."[22]

Not satisfied to stick to Indulgences, Luther, although he had promised his bishop he would not publish these errors, went on to condemn Purgatory and attack the Church's teachings on Grace and Justification. His Archbishop commissioned professors from the University of Mayence to examine Luther's theses. After painstaking study and much deliberation, the conclusion they all arrived at was that the teachings were totally heretical and Luther was to be censored. Wanting to maintain smooth relations with Pope Leo X, until he was ready to act, Luther wrote the Pope a letter professing his loyalty, explaining what he had written and his willingness to wait upon his decision.

"They are disputations, not doctrines, not dogmas, set out as usual in an enigmatic form; yet could I have foreseen it, I should certainly have taken part on my side, that they should be more easy to understand." "...most blessed Father, I offer myself prostrate at the feet of your Holiness and give myself up to you with all that I am or have; quicken, slay, call, recall, approve, reprove, as shall please thee. It rests with your Holiness to promote or prevent my undertaking, to declare it right or wrong. Whatever happens, I recognize the voice of your Holiness as that of Christ abiding and speaking in thee. If I deserve death, I do not refuse to die."[23]

The Pope called for Luther to appear in Rome and answer the charges against him. But when the Elector of Saxony[24] requested the matter be handled in his country, the Pope bowed to the king's wishes and allowed Luther to meet with Cardinal St. Cajetan, a legate well respected by Rome and Germany alike. At that meeting, Luther challenged the Cardinal, demanding he be shown where he was in error. The Cardinal mentioned two specific errors contained in the theses: *The Treasures of the Church from which the Pope* grants *Indulgences are not the merits of Christ and of the Saints."* and *"That faith alone was sufficient for salvation."*

Upon receipt of the Cardinal's findings, Luther quickly dispatched a letter to the Pope in Rome, indicating he never *"intended to teach anything offensive to Catholic teaching, to the Holy Scriptures, to the authority of the Fathers, or to the decree of the Pope."* He did not wait the three day stay he had requested, but instead hurriedly departed for Augsburg, Germany. When he arrived, he immediately posted an appeal on the gates of the Carmelite monastery where he was lodging, in defense of his attack on Indulgences, explaining he was compelled to attack them as they were not of God! Luther refuted the findings of the Cardinal. Accusing his judges of being untrustworthy, he justified his refusal to go to Rome complaining: *"where justice once abided, homicide now dwelt."*[25]

The Pope did not give up on Luther; he sent another emissary to resolve the problem. After the meeting, Luther responded by writing to the Pope yet another letter, promising his undying faithfulness and obedience, insisting he never wished to hurt the Roman Catholic Church or usurp the Pope's authority. He further professed that he accepted the Church as having the final say; and that nothing in Heaven and on earth is superior to the Church, except Jesus Christ Himself. How much did that mean? The ink is hardly dry; Luther follows that with, and I quote,

"I have often said that hitherto I have only been playing. Now at last we shall act seriously against Roman authority and Roman arrogance."[26]

Not only did he betray his promise to the Pope, he told a friend that he was not sure if the Pope was not the antichrist himself or his apostle.

It was difficult to determine which was the real philosophy of Luther, his protestations of loyalty or his continuing attacks on the teachings of the Church. He grew more and more arrogant, casting aspersions on Dogma after Dogma, insisting there was no room in God's church for:

Indulgences;

Confession;

Purgatory;

praying to the Saints as there are no Saints - they retained the sins of corruption for all eternity, except their corruption was covered by the cloak of Jesus' merits.

Whether he realized it or not, he firmly began to preach *predestination*: that we had inherited the sins of our fallen parents - Adam and Eve, and that all our actions - good and bad were highly offensive to God. With this philosophy, was he not preaching hopelessness which could only lead to despair?

Then to keep everyone from running from him, like frightened deer, he declared that:

"all Christians are priests, all have equal authority to interpret the Bible for themselves, and there is no difference among the baptized, priest, bishop, pope."[27]

Now he had to get on the good side of the princes whose support he was endeavoring to gain, so he declared:

"For as much as the temporal power is ordained of God to punish the wicked and protect the good, therefore it must be allowed to do its work unhindered on the whole Christian body, without respect to persons, whether it strike popes, bishops, priests, monks, nuns, or whom it will. The secular power should summon a 'free council' which should reorganize the constitution of the Church from its foundation and must liberate Germany from the Roman robbers, from the devilish rule of the Romans."[28]

If that is not bad enough, he further boldly stated:

"There is no finer government in the world than that of the Turks, who have neither a spiritual nor a secular

code of law, but only their Koran. And it must be acknowledged that there is no more disagreeable system of rule than ours, with our Canon Law and our Common Law, while no class any longer obeys either natural reason or Holy Scripture." [29]

Pope Leo X, always endeavoring to keep his family together, wrote:

"Imitating the clemency of the Almighty Who wills not the death of a sinner, but that he should be converted and live, we shall forget all injuries done to us and the Apostolic See, and we shall do all we can to make him give up his errors. By the depths of God's mercy and the Blood of Our Lord Jesus Christ, shed for the Redemption of man and the foundation of the Church, we expect and pray Luther and his followers to cease disturbing the peace, the unity, and the power of the Church." [30]

The Pope gave Luther 60 days to denounce his heretical teachings. Luther's bold pride would not allow him to admit he had been in error. The Pope excommunicated him. It is said, *There is no furor like a woman scorned*; well I would have to add, *Nor like a heretic who has been chastised.* Luther responded by immediately publishing an arrogant denunciation of the Holy See, entitled: *"Against the Execrable Bull of the Antichrist."* He ranted on and on, exclaiming:

"...thanks to the zeal of my friends I have seen this bat in all its beauty." "I maintain that the author of this Bull is the Antichrist: I curse it as a blasphemy against the Son of God...I trust that every Christian who accepts this Bull will suffer the torments of Hell." "Leo X and you, the Roman Cardinals, I tell you to your faces...Renounce your Satanic blasphemies against Jesus Christ." [31]

To add insult to injury, Luther publicly burned the

Pope's Bull, along with the writings of St. Thomas Aquinas and varied Catholic theologians. He said that he wished it had been the Pope and the See that he had burned. Then in a half crazed fury, he exploded: *"If you do not separate from Rome, there is no salvation for your souls."*[32]

And with all this, this excommunicated priest continued to celebrate Mass, his congregation unaware they were no longer Catholic. He infected them with his heresies that they accepted as Dogmas of the Church (as he, a priest had espoused them). No wonder Teresa of Avila said Luther would be the *last* to enter the gates of Heaven.

Luther, who came out so strongly against all authority of the Church, became an authority unto himself, granting dispensations at will, when it was convenient to do so and beneficial to him and his desires, like the time he dispensed himself and Katherine Von Bora[33] from their vows of celibacy. He further took away the holiness of the Sacrament of Marriage, proclaiming: *"If the mistress of the house is unwilling, let the maid come."* He granted a special dispensation to Philip of Hess, allowing him to live a bigamous relationship.

Luther fell victim to the very thing he had preached against - pride! As a professor, he had taught that the principle characteristic and sin of heretics is pride. Now he was guilty of the very evil that led to the *original* fall - pride! Did he not remember when he had said:

"In their pride they insist on their own opinions. Frequently they serve God with great fervor, and they do not intend any evil; but they serve God according to their own will...Even when refuted, they are ashamed to retract their errors and to change their words...They think they are guided directly by God ...The things that have been established for centuries, and for which so many martyrs have suffered death, they begin to treat as doubtful questions."[34]

How did it happen? When did it begin?

In trying to discover why Luther did what he did, why it happened and when, we need to reflect: Could it possibly have happened *before* he went to Rome? Could it have started when he found his duties as a monk interfering with his *humanistic* interests: pursuits of intellectual and worldly knowledge? Did he just go through the motions, performing his religious duties more than a little grudgingly and haphazardly? Did it start when, for the sake of doing something he judged important, he failed to recite the Divine Office for three to four weeks at a time,[35] although he was bound to say his Office daily under the penalty of grievous sin? Did he not know that this act of *obedience* was serious, second only to the observance of his vows? Was it because of some task he felt more pressing or was it part of his unwillingness to conform? Was he above obeying? And maybe, to people not bound under these sets of rules, it may seem petty or foolish, but the word is *obedience, and bowing humbly to the wisdom of those whom God has put in charge!*

Luther later wrote, he had led the *strictest life* of a monk, and when he felt remorse at having disobeyed his Rule, he excessively recited the Office to the point of exhaustion, in an effort to make up for his disobedience. Did he do this out of love of the Lord or fear? Only Luther and his Lord know the answer. But an insight into Luther might be at his ordination. When his father asked him *why* he had chosen to become a priest, he replied he was afraid God would have struck him dead if he had not. Is this the God of Love we hear Luther later espousing, the God of freedom?

Luther considered himself the worst of sinners and did penance to such self-prescribed excesses he said himself, it was suicidal. Struggles he had with the *Church* had little to do with Luther's turning against his religion. Some writers believe it was his haunting need to placate the torturous doubts he *inwardly* suffered as to the salvation of his soul; he sought constant reassurance that he was redeemed of (what he judged were) his unforgivable sins. Luther, obsessed by these thoughts, tortured himself with his fear of predestination[36] and his desperate need to know that he was one of those predestined to be saved. Trying to bargain with God, laying the blame at His Feet, Luther grasped and held onto the *heretical teaching* of two priests, John Wycliff and John Hus, that man was not born with *"free will"* although this heresy was condemned in 1410.

It is written that Luther was an *intelligent* priest. Did he put himself above the traditional teachings of the Church, above God's representative, the Pope, as he endeavored to grasp at *God's* knowledge of right or wrong? As Adam and Eve before him sought to know more than God had revealed to them by eating of the fruit of the Tree of Knowledge, was Luther seeking this illusive wisdom in a tree called Conscience? Was he, in his pride, looking for insights not passed on by the Holy Spirit through the Catholic Church?

Luther was tortured by doubts of his vocation. There seemed to be an endless turbulence in his life, with him being tossed about by waves of hatred, envy and pride that resulted in violent fits of temper. Had the Lord given him so many gifts, Luther forgot *Who* was the Giver and *who* was the recipient? Relying on himself, was he deafened by *the enemy* telling him he could work it out; that the way to work it out was to realize it was not his fault but the system, and the system was the Church he had vowed to live and die for? When he reflected back on his days as a monk, he said:

"From misplaced reliance on my righteousness, my heart became full of distrust, doubt, fear, hatred, and blasphemy of God. I was such an enemy of Christ on His Cross, I loathed the sight and shut my eyes and felt

that I would have rather seen the devil. My spirit was broken and I was always in a state of melancholy; for, do what I would, my righteousness and my `good works' brought me no help or consolation. "[37]

Within these words, which come from Luther himself, lies the reason for so many tragic happenings that have come to pass. *Take him off the Cross!* Like the devil at the foot of the Cross, Luther could not stand to look upon Jesus on the Cross. He *loathed* the sight of Our Lord on the Cross, the sight of the Precious Lamb Who suffered and died for him. He said, he would have rather seen the devil! My God, had the enemy planted the seed of sin within his heart, as he had with Judas when he too left to betray his Lord? Had sin taken over his soul, and because he had no respite from his melancholy through his *good works*[38] that he came out against St. James and his words:

"Take the case, my brothers, of someone who has never done a single good act but claims that he has faith. Will that faith save him? If one of the brothers or one of the sisters is in need of clothes and has not enough to food to live on, and one of you says to them, `I wish you well; keep yourself warm and eat plenty,' without giving them these bare necessities of life, then what good is that? Faith is like that: if good works do not go with it, it is quite dead.

"This is the way to talk to people of that kind: `You say you have faith and I have good deeds; I will prove to you that I have faith by showing you my good deeds - now you prove to me that you have faith without any good deeds to show. You believe in the One God - that is credible enough, but the demons have the same belief, and they tremble with fear. Do realize, you senseless man, that faith without good deeds is useless. You surely know that Abraham our father was justified by his deed,

because he offered his son Issac on the altar? There you see it: faith and deeds were working together; his faith became perfect by what he did. This is what Scripture means when it says: Abraham put his faith in God, and this was counted as making him justified; and that is why he was called the friend of God.'"[39]

Not only did he come out against *good works*, and we thought that was the reason Luther took James' Letter out of his rendition of the Bible,[40] but now we can see it could have been to justify himself and the reason he turned against Mother Church. As you read the rest of James' Letter are you, too, wondering; if Luther read a condemnation upon himself rather than a loving challenge, in James words:

"Consider it all joy, my brothers, when you encounter various trials, for you know that the testing of your faith produces perseverance."[41] and then again: *"But let him ask in **faith**, with no doubting, for he who doubts is like a wave of the sea that is driven and tossed about by the wind."*[42]

"...The brother in lowly circumstances should take pride in his high standing, and the rich one in his lowliness, for he will pass away `like the flower of the field."[43]

"...Blessed is the man who perseveres in temptation, for when he has been proved, he will receive the crown of life that He promises to those who love Him."[44]

Luther came out against the Ten Commandments, too. What was his thinking, that he was, according to him, not answerable for any sins he may have committed; after all he and everyone else was born without *free will*? So, did the Ten Commandments call him to accountability, just as St. James letters did? He came out against Moses and the Old Law which Jesus came to fulfill. Was he saying: *If the law condemns me or calls me to live differently, change the law*

*or discredit it? If I cannot honor the Sacraments do away
with them? If I cannot live by the Ten Commandments,
condemn them? If I cannot obey the Church, change it?*

Luther not only removed James' Letter, he changed
the Word of God so brutally, Protestant scholars say it was
an abomination. Had he forgotten the words of St. Paul:

*"And though we, or an Angel from Heaven, preach
a Gospel to you, beside that which we have preached
to you, let him be anathema.*[45] *If anyone preaches you
a Gospel besides that which you have received, let him
be anathema."*[46]

In 1515, Martin Luther was to attack the very
Foundations of the Catholic Church using the *selling of
Indulgences* as a knife which would pierce the Heart of Jesus
Crucified and the Church which flowed from that Heart. As
a result, not only would the Catholic world never be the
same, but the very essence of Christianity would change for
all time. Opening the door to more conflicts to this very
day, this one act of disobedience was to lead to the scandal
of over 40,000[47] splinters of the Cross of Jesus. What with
disobedience building on disobedience, and dissension
building on dissension, the unity Jesus commanded, *"as I
am one with the Father,"* has instead become Christian
against Christian, brother against brother. And how our
Beloved Lord weeps.

The saddest part is that Luther did not intend for the
Church to split and be fragmented. He was not trying to
start another religion, as Calvin did. When Pride and
Humility knocked on the door of his heart, Luther opened
the door to Pride instead of Humility and all the other evil
spirits came rushing in. St. Teresa of Avila said that creeping
earthworms of evil can sneak even into the rooms of the
Interior Castle, where one seeks unity with God. Teresa
spoke of the temptations and dangers of *beginners* who

would reform others before completely reforming themselves. Now, in no way, are we making the presumptive judgment that Luther was a beginner; but reading his life, one can see him doing just that, reforming others before disciplining himself, attacking without thinking of the consequences, *he* doing the reforming instead of God, *his* the work, not *His!*

The Church is perfect, because it is Christ's Church, and Christ is perfect. But when we see abuses there is such an urgency to correct these problems that arise because of the frailty of some of the pastors who have inherited the care of Jesus' lambs and sheep, we, like Peter, rush in, lopping off ears whereas Christ is saying: *"I'll take care of My Church."* Luther saw injustices, weaknesses and abuses, the Church permeated by self-interest. But instead of turning to prayer - *"the sword which cuts the million of favors hanging from Heaven on silken cords,"*[48] and waiting upon the Lord, he allowed another *big* enemy - *Anger* to take over. He did not heed the Word, he so staunchly proclaimed as the final authority, where Jesus said to Peter who had lopped off the ear of the high priest's servant:

"Put back your sword where it belongs. Those who use the sword are sooner or later destroyed by it. Do you not suppose I can call upon My Father to provide at a moment's notice more than twelve legions of angels?"[49]

There were abuses that needed reform, not revolution! We are speaking of *men's* errors, not the Church's. When Jesus chose Peter whom He knew would deny Him three times, He was plainly declaring that even if a Pope acted unwisely, hell would not prevail against His Church, that He would be with her until the end of time. And under the protection of the Holy Spirit, no Pope, no matter his worthiness or unworthiness, has ever made an error in Faith and Morals!

Now, in the time of Luther, as in centuries past, there were heads of state choosing members of their families to occupy such high positions in the Church as that of Cardinal,[50] inheriting not only titles but lands that went with the office, smacking clearly of *nepotism* and interference of State with Church. For a matter of fact, that law about separation of Church and State was originally instituted to protect the Church from abuses from the State (such as these) not protection of the State from the Church.

Now there was another problem - politics! The nobility of Luther's day *used him to accomplish their own designs,* and that was taking over the lands of the Papacy. So often, when someone offers to help us, if we are not careful, we will discover they are using *us* to help *them.* And so it was with Luther and the German princes!

Who was Luther?

Luther was born into a period of rebirth or *Renaissance.*[51] For a thousand years there had been virtually no books written, no paintings, no buildings - only wars. People were so busy protecting themselves, few of them had time for learning. For that reason the Middle Ages are often called the *Dark Ages. "Only the Catholic Church in its abbeys and monasteries, kept learning alive."*[52] This Renaissance that had begun in Italy in the Fourteenth Century, was to be a reawakening of culture and art, and it was to be a glorious period. The problem was that in seeking this new dawn, they turned to civilizations which had perished from decadence and ungodliness, those of the Ancient Roman and Greek civilizations. As these civilizations before them, this period had little respect for Christianity, claiming it did not allow freedom of decision-making or actions. It did not allow for literal license. They wanted freedom, and they would go to any lengths to accomplish their purpose, even to the destruction of their souls and the souls of others. In contrast to the philosophy of that period, the end justified the means *humanism,* St. Teresa, infused by knowledge from our Lord Jesus, wrote:

"My intention was good-but the act was wrong; for to accomplish a good, however great it may be, even a small evil is not to be done."

Humanism was so obviously the work of the *serpent,* the whole philosophy centered on *self:* on *man,* on *his* ability, *his* intellect, and *his* power; the devil promising that through the development of *man's* mind and body he could control his own life, in a nutshell - *Pride!* *Humanism* slowly, deviously turned men away from faith in God to reliance on man; and this subtly resulted in Christians worshiping man instead of God. Whenever you hear, *"I believe in man,"* remember in the Book of Revelations when Michael the Archangel threw out Satan crying the War Cry: *Who is like God!* Recall as well how Adam and Eve were lured away from the Loving Arms of God by the promise they could be like gods; *man* could be like gods.

Oh, the *evil one* had help, as always. The Church in the Renaissance was debilitated by men within the Church who practiced *nepotism, nationalism, and humanism*; they were choking the Church with their self-seeking, malignant tentacles of greed and power. Satan took this fuel and added it to the fire of discontent. Yes there was corruption within the Church. But was this not the reason Jesus chose twelve men, one of whom would betray Him and one deny Him, with all but one running away from Him and the Cross? Was not Jesus saying, no matter how unworthy the instruments, no matter how unwisely the inheritors of the kingdom acted, He would protect His Church and she would survive until the end of time?

Luther - his story

Statue of Luther, Calvin and Protestant leaders in Worms, Germany

St. Augustine wrote: *"Love God and do whatever you wish."* the idea being that if you love God you will desire nothing but to love Him and because of that love for Him you will not desire to sin against Him, for every sin is against God as it wounds Him so. Luther scandalously wrote to the embarrassment of Lutherans till today, *"Be a sinner, and sin boldly; but believe more boldly."*

Augustine went from sin to holiness. Luther went from holiness to sin. What went wrong? Both men were slated for greatness. One bought fame and became infamous. The other, like St. Peter before him, repented of his sins[53] and became an early Father of the Church.

"Luther rode through his century like a demon crushing under his feet what a thousand years had venerated."[54]

In their search for the truth, Protestant writers have unearthed a different Luther than the almost fictional life that has been passed down through the years, since that fateful day he posted those 95 theses against the Church.

"How small the Reformer has become according to the Luther studies of our own Protestant investigators! How his merits have shriveled up! We believed that we owed to him the spirit of toleration and liberty of conscience. Not in the least! We recognized in his translation of the Bible a masterpiece stamped with the impress[55] *of originality - we may be happy now if it is plainly called a plagiarism.*[56] *We venerated him as the father of the popular school system - a*

purely fictitious greatness which we have no right to claim for him! We imagined that we found in Luther's words splendid suggestions for a rational treatment of poverty and that a return to him would bring us back to the true principles of charity - but the laurels do not belong to him, they must be conceded to the Catholic Church. "[57]

As we review Luther's life, making further references to writings and discoveries of Protestants who loved him and his memory, we pause to commend the courage and humility they had to admit Luther, their hero, was not all they had believed and taught. We quote:

"He attempted reformation and ended in deformation." [58]

In seeking the truth, many have been led to believe in the myth that is Luther, not the reality. Because of that they have had prejudices passed down from one generation to the next, since the Sixteenth Century, making the unity of Jesus' beloved family - impossible! Repeating the *lies and falsehoods* of the past, they continue to:

- scandalize the Priesthood,
- repeat stories of the cruelty of nuns and their lifestyle,
- call the Pope the Anti-Christ,
- call the spotless Bride of Christ, the Catholic Church, the *"great harlot of the Apocalypse," "the mother of fornication and the abominations of the earth."*

Every lie and falsehood that has been used to defame the Catholic Church can trace its roots to Luther, its original inventor. [59] This is not a condemnation of our brothers and sisters in Christ; they are the product of how they were taught from infancy by their families and by preachers who unknowingly, wrongfully passed down this bigotry which has been an instrument of division, pitting brother against brother.

We are writing this chapter to clear up misunderstandings so that, at the least, we may know one another better; for you cannot love someone you do not know; it is ignorance, not knowledge that separates and kills the opportunity God gives us to love one another.[60]

Archbishop Fulton J. Sheen said:

"Hundreds hate what the Church stands for, but thousands hate her for what they think she stands for."[61]

Those who malign the Church must be made aware of the truth, and then if they wish to continue doing so the responsibility is theirs alone; they alone will stand before the throne of God and answer Jesus' question to Saul:

"...why do you persecute me?"[62]

When you are confronted by well-meaning and not so well-meaning brothers and sisters in Christ, it is important that you ask them the following questions.

- Can you tell me what you believe, or is what you believe that which your founders have rejected from the Church founded by Christ?

- Do you know what was so heretical in Luther's teachings that caused him to be excommunicated?

- Do you know the difference between Luther's teachings and those of Christ?

- Why did Luther denounce the Church's teachings on *good works* and change Paul's Scripture to read "Salvation through Faith alone,"[63] adding *alone*; it was never included in the Bible before Luther?

- Why did Luther declare that each man could interpret Scripture for himself, according to his conscience, and yet he insisted his followers *accept his* new Bible as the word of God? And when they refused, disobeyed him, and became their own individual ministers, why did he berate them, calling them *"a debauched people" "given over to all kinds of vices?"* If he was filled with such love for them, he wanted to set them free from the tentacles of the Papacy, why did he refer to those whom St. Paul would have called *beloved,*[64] *as "abominable hogs"?*

As we go on, you will discover, along with us, the many changes Luther brought about which ultimately backfired on him. As we said at the beginning of this chapter, in no way would we desire to hurt any of our dear and holy brothers and sisters who are Lutheran, or Protestant of any kind, but we must speak out; for if we were not to do so, as Jesus said *"...the stones would cry out!"*[65] The Schism resulting from one man's act of dissidence spread like a dangerous plague and infected 6,000,000 Catholics in Europe, most of whom were unaware they were no longer Catholic. As Luther was a priest, and to a Catholic, the word of a priest was like God Himself speaking, *heresy became truth*, the lambs strayed and were lost for 500 years. But they are coming back. And we will be *one body* partaking of the one Bread of Life! This is our prayer and this is what this book is truly about.

Please, if you are not Catholic, or if you were turned away from Mother Church, pray to the Holy Spirit to open your mind and heart to hear what He may be saying to you. Remember that the Catholic Church was not begun by man, but Christ Himself. She is the work of His Hands, not of man's. She is the beloved Spouse that Christ chose for Himself, promising that hell would not prevail against her.[66] You may recall that Jesus said that the Shepherd would give his life for his sheep, not the hireling who would run away. As the Church is His Church, when you follow His Church, you follow Him. When you leave His Church, you leave Him[67] to follow His hireling.[68] The Catholic Church is the only one which flowed from the Heart of Christ and has continued to flow out to the whole world, uninterrupted for 2000 years, in spite of attacks from without and within.

To those of you who have fallen away from the Catholic Church into which you were baptized, it is important to remember that Christ bequeathed (left) the Church to Peter and the first bishops, directing them to pass on all that He had taught them. Therefore anyone who knowingly leaves this Church, which Jesus founded for our salvation, and through his *own* fault dies outside of the Church, will not obtain the salvation promised by Jesus, the salvation that is our inheritance from Our Savior Who died on the Cross for us. Does this sound harsh and unloving? We do not mean it to be, but better that we make you angry with us than have God hurt by the loss of you with Him in Paradise. We just repeat what that great Doctor of the Church - St. Augustine said:

"No one can be saved who has not Christ for his head, and no one can have Christ for his head who does not belong to His body, the Church."

Augustine said that in the Fourth Century, when we were all one Church. We read in Holy Scripture that Jesus told Peter, our first Pope that he was the Rock upon which He would build *His Church*.[69] So it is plain that St. Augustine is referring to the only Church that existed at his time, and from the time of Jesus. Our problem with Luther is he was a priest and an Augustinian. He knew what the Church teaches; he learned about the Church from the teachings of one of the *great* Church Fathers to whose Order he belonged - St. Augustine. Now, we ask you was he not pridefully placing himself above *the* Divine Founder Jesus and his earthly founder Augustine, both of whom he had vowed to obey? In the next chapter on Henry VIII and the Church of England, you will see how Luther's Forty One propositions[70] influenced the Church of England's original Forty-two Articles, which were cut down to Thirty-eight and are used till today.

Luther and Justification through Faith alone

As the misconceptions that spread throughout the Christian world began with a man of God who went astray, so it is important that we right the misconceptions that have permeated and divided Christians since the days of Luther, by men of God who are unwittingly transmitting lies about the Catholic Faith and what we believe. We want to briefly make right the wrongs, as we go on with the life of Luther.

First of all, we do not believe that we can achieve *justification* solely through the intercession of Mother Mary, or the Saints, nor do we believe that we can achieve *justification* through our own merit, through our good works alone. We believe that our Salvation comes through the merits of Jesus Christ and His Sacrifice on the Cross.

We do not believe (as they allege), that we can bring about our own Justification and Sanctification by *solely* thing-doing, even good thing-doing, pleasing acts to the Father such as fasting, attending Holy Mass, performing acts of mortification and penance. When these actions, which can be holy, are done out of fear, or for personal gain rather than out of love for Jesus, they are not precious to the Heart of God. God does not do for us out of design, but out of love. Can we do less?

Through His Grace, we are inspired to do good works. When we fast, we can share in some small way Jesus' days on the Mount of Temptation. Furthermore, Jesus told the Apostles that this was the only way that certain spirits[71] could be dispelled, and there has always been need to fight the fallen angels who are ever-ready to attack. We attend Holy Mass, to walk beside Jesus and stand at the foot of the Cross during this ongoing Sacrifice of the Cross - the Sacrifice of the Mass, to receive Him so that we can be made perfect as the Father is perfect,[72] and behold His Beatific Vision some day.

Luther decided that man was evil because of the sins of Adam and Eve, that he was so corrupted by his first parents, he had no free will to love God or anyone and consequently could not do any good thing. He taught that the taint of sin and corruption hung over man incapacitating him, blocking him from performing acts pleasing to God. He further went on that as man was conceived in sin by sinners (as he taught all mankind was sinful), so the babe within his mother's womb was sinning and incurring damnation before he was even born. He was so obsessed by this belief in predestination that he was manic, worrying whether he was one of those chosen who were saved. Imagine the self-doubts because he had no control at all over the outcome of his life, and could not participate in his salvation. He called man a bad tree that could not bear good fruit. He said that man could not help committing sin. He said:

"Man may do his best to do good, still his every action is unavoidably bad; he commits a sin as often as he draws a breath."

"No action that was bad would bring the regenerate[73] man under condemnation, because he was justified by faith; nor were his good actions, in even the slightest degree meritorious, because they were done entirely through the grace given him by the Holy Ghost."

"The nature of man is so corrupted that it can never be regenerated, and sin will remain in his soul, even of the just, forever. God's all-powerful grace does not cleanse from sin. The Almighty does not regard the sins of men. He covers them with the merits of Christ and does not impute them to the sinner whose faith in the sufferings of the Redeemer is made manifest. This is the faith that tends to prevent our filth from stinking before God."[74]

Luther also said that the Christian needs only to believe in the Gospel and in Jesus Christ to be saved, and through this faith his sins are forgiven and he receives divine grace. This he receives from the Holy Spirit Who works solely through the Word of God - the Bible; and man's cooperation cannot alter it in any way, shape, or form. He has nothing to do with it! If a man believes in Jesus Christ as his personal Savior, he is automatically saved, no matter what he does. It does not matter what he has ever done in his life, whether he has repented of his sins, whether on his death bed he asks for forgiveness, whether he is in a state of grace, by his faith he is saved.[75] I wonder if anyone would have the guts to tell survivors of the Holocaust that Hitler was saved? Or maybe serial killers? How about child molesters?

By this teaching Luther contradicted Christ Himself. The Lord taught the people the two most important Commandments. In both these Commandments Jesus speaks of love. That's an action on our part! Christ said *love* not faith! He said you shall *love* the Lord in the first and you shall *love* your neighbor in the second! He did not say *faith*; He said *love*! In Holy Scripture, we read:

"And one of them, a lawyer, asked Him a question, to test Him. `Teacher, which is the greatest Commandment in the law?' And He said to him, `You shall love the Lord your God with all your heart, and with all your soul, and with all your mind. This is the greatest and first commandment. And a second is like it, You shall love your neighbor as yourself. On these two commandments depend the law and the prophets.'"[76]

Luther not only wanted to do away with the Law, but Moses, as well. The Ten Commandments had been given to Moses by God Himself, and Moses in submission to the Lord, gave them to the Israelites. Moses passed on the words of *God*, not his words, not *his* commandments, but God's. He was calling the Israelites to obey Yahweh's[77]

Commandments, the Divine Law from above. As Moses insisted on the strict observance of the Law, Luther had to discredit him, saying Moses only had jurisdiction over the Jews, not the Christians. Calling him an enemy of Christ, Luther said that Moses was to be looked *"upon even as a heretic, ex-communicated, damned, worse than the Pope and the devil."*

Luther spoke of the Law being incompatible with the Gospel and yet Jesus said: *"Do not think that I have come to destroy the Law or the prophets. I come not to destroy, but to fulfill."*[78] Jewish converts to Christianity all say that it was the Gospel fulfillment of the Old Testament that brought them to Jesus and His Church.

Luther warned his followers not to allow the Law to influence their consciences. [This would backfire on him, later on when he would call them unmanageable "pigs" and worse than they were under the Pope.] Luther said that God used the Law as a hammer to show man that he is absolutely incapable of obeying it; and then further crippled his followers with a doctrine that proposed *"the impossibility of doing good and that he (man) should learn to despair of himself."*[79] This is not only illogical, it is completely contrary to the God we know and love. He is suggesting that God would give us laws that were impossible to obey and consequently we would be doomed to fail. That sounds like Lucifer, not God. What good earthly father would cause his children to fail? If he who is a sinner would not deceive his children, how more so would *God* not impose laws impossible to obey, leading them to despair? This is a sin that is unforgivable, that of despair. Luther knew better than to accuse God of causing man to commit an unforgivable sin.

Again we hear, as with others who have strayed away from the Truth, the enemy of God using Luther as an instrument of his lies. Do we not hear in Luther's words an echo of the serpent's words to Eve in the Garden of Eden when he called God a liar, insisting that God knew that eating from the Tree of Knowledge would not harm them but instead open them to the knowledge of good and evil? When Luther taught that man did not need to follow the tenets of the Faith[80] which were passed down to us from not only the Apostles but the Prophets before them, that man could determine what was right and wrong by his own *conscience*, was he not espousing the devil's philosophy and not God's?

Luther and his visits from the devil

Luther, according to his own testimony, had many conversations with the devil. He said that the devil comes to men disguised as Christ, and changes into *"an angel of light"* so that he can frighten us with the Law.

But then, in another reference to the enemy of God, Luther writes that the devil appeared to him one evening at midnight and spoke to him with such a terrifying deeply guttural rasping voice, he almost frightened him half to death. He wrote that his heart beat so rapidly, he thought it would burst within his chest; his fear, raging inside him like a volcano, exploding, erupting rivers of sweat to pour down his face.

He said that the devil told him in no uncertain terms that he was to refute the Mass, Mary, and the Saints, and gave him his highest stamp of approval on his (Luther's) *"justification by faith alone."* He continued to testify that he had no doubt it was Satan himself who spoke, directing him to speak against the Mother of God, the Holy Mass and the Saints.[81] Now who could follow someone who said that he derived his authority from Lucifer? But yet, many dear sincere Christians proclaim the doctrines of Luther, not knowing they emanated from the mandate he received from the enemy of God.

Jesus said: *"Unless you eat my Body and drink My Blood you have no life in you."*[82] Is this not a call to action, a call to cooperate with His Grace? If we were not called to play a part in His Plan of salvation for us, why did He warn, *"those who lead my children astray, better they be born with a millstone around their neck?*[83] If man is hopelessly condemned or saved automatically before birth, then can he be led astray?

The Lord throughout Scripture, tells us *how* to be closer to God and how to achieve eternal life. When the rich young man came to Jesus and asked Him how he could inherit the Kingdom of God, Jesus did not say "have faith;" He said, *"If you would enter life, keep the Commandments."* [84] He told him what to do and not do; these are all works, action:

"You shall not kill

"You shall not commit adultery

"You shall not steal

"You shall not bear false witness

"Honor your father and mother

"You shall love your neighbor as yourself."

When the young man protested he had done all these things, Jesus told him to *sell* all he had, give it to the poor and follow Him. This is plainly Jesus calling the young man to participate in His *Salvific*[85] Grace.

Now, Luther preached *sola scriptura.*[86] What happened? How did he come to terms with the many references in Scripture where Jesus spoke of *action* on our part? Did he wipe out, or did he change the Scripture where Jesus said *"Take up My yoke upon you, and learn from Me, for I am meek and humble of heart; and you shall find rest to your souls?"*[87]

This does not sound like a God who has hopelessness planned for our future; nor does this sound like a Lord Who is saying, *"Just sit back and do nothing; it has all been decided."* If we read the Bible, we cannot fail to recognize the discrepancies between what Luther is preaching and what God is saying in His Word. This misguided ambassador-of-Christ, who changed and cut the Word to accommodate his own brand of religion, did what St. John said would condemn him:

> *"This is my solemn warning to all who hear the prophecies in this book: if anyone adds anything to them, God will add to him every plague mentioned in the book; if anyone cuts anything out of the prophecies in this book, God will cut off his share of the Tree of Life and of the holy city, which are described in the book."*[88]

Luther was obsessed with *thoughts* of lust - which led to sin; and sin always wanting company - led others to sin. Jesus said; *"If your eye offends you, pluck it out. Better you enter the Kingdom without an eye than to wind up in Gehenna."*[89] Luther recounted, in his book *Table Talk*, how a young man came to him and shared that his conscience was troubling him, to the point of causing him to have bouts with despair. Luther said it was the devil taunting him; and when he had these thoughts, he should go out, have a good time and drink heavily - even sin! In this way he would castigate *Lucifer*, block him from filling his head with sorrow over having sinned and stop him from harassing him with warnings to guard against committing future sins. He wrote that when the devil plagued him with such thoughts of scrupulosity, he would drink more, eat more, carry on more, indulge his every desire and in this way infuriate the devil. I should think he would accomplish just the opposite! Luther said that his followers were to put aside, most especially, the Ten Commandments which the devil uses to badger us.

Luther and his plan to do away with the Papacy

To appeal to the masses, and usurp the God-given authority of the "Barque[90] of Peter" Luther promulgated a theology heretofore never proclaimed, that of the individual determining right from wrong according to his own conscience. When he attacked the authority of the Vicar of Christ, he attacked the foster father left by Jesus Himself to head and guide His Family, the Church - His Mystical Body on earth. Had Jesus seen this prideful act which would lead so many innocent lambs astray, in the Garden of Gethsemane? Was this part of the pain that caused Him to shed tears mingled with blood and water? Was this cup of disunity and disobedience the cup that He pleaded with the Father to *make pass from Him?*[91]

What happens when the children have no earthly father to help them discern right from wrong? You have chaos - a household filled with members wildly going their own way, doing their own thing. Numb to the possibility of suffering later consequences, oblivious to the inevitable end result of disunity stemming from their self-seeking, they go on blocking out all that they know to be holy for temporary gratification and the aftermath is the family falls apart! Jesus said *"A house divided against itself will not stand."*[92] This is what happened with Luther!

Although he began by proposing man follow and formulate his beliefs based on his own understanding and reasoning, Luther soon changed his tune, proclaiming *himself* the final word! He began to believe that he was above not only the Popes but all the Councils called down through the ages. He placed himself as *the authority*, accusing those who opposed him and his own brand of church as he saw it *"untrustworthy teachers, dolts, asses and infernal blasphemers."*[93] He attacked Defenders of the Faith who had faithfully passed down the teachings of the Church for centuries, calling them *"pools out of which Christians have been drinking impure and loathsome water."*[94] He accused holy writers: Saints Jerome, John Chrysostom, Augustine, Thomas Aquinas, Basil, and Cyprian, to mention a few, of having fallen into error. Claiming these holy Doctors of the Church had been deceived by the devil, and because of their lack of knowledge of the Bible had rained down immeasurable harm upon the innocent, they *"deserved to be in hell rather than in heaven."*[95]

He alone was in the right! Friends became enemies when they would or could not accept his extremely controversial teachings. Early Church Fathers whom he had previously respected, he labeled: *"rascals, beasts, antichrists,"*[96] adding they were *"unworthy of a hearing."* As he alone had the doctrines from Heaven, he elected himself *"Doctor of doctors,"*[97] whom all must obey or suffer the pain of being *"everlastingly condemned."*[98]

How was Luther able to delude so many faithful members of the True Church to leave her and how has his influence survived 500 years, with righteous and very holy people following him? He began twisting and changing the doctrines of the Church in order to disguise the heresies he was feeding the innocent. These precious doctrines that had come from the very beginning, constant and unchanged for centuries, were aborted and scarred by Luther, to cast scandal on the Church founded by Christ and the Supreme Head of the Church chosen by Christ. Calling all Popes the antichrist, Luther said he would outlive them and bring about their death, once and for all.

Luther seemed to be vacillating constantly; first advocating then attacking that which he had formerly professed. One day, the Church was infallible; the next day she was fallible. He insisted all should obey the Councils of the Church and then demanded they ignore them. When it was convenient, he ascertained the government had complete jurisdiction over all ministers of Religion and then disavowed it. One moment he was speaking conclusively of the reality of the existence of hell and the next questioning whether it existed at all. He would teach the Sacraments conferred Grace upon those who receive them and then that they do not. He went from claiming there were seven Sacraments to denying all but two. Then Luther increased the number of Sacraments to five. He upheld the Church's teaching of the Seven Sacraments and then denied five again! At one point he taught that Grace was conferred upon the child (or person) being Baptized and then that there was no effect upon the recipient's soul. He taught that the stain of Original Sin which we inherited from our first parents' Adam and Eve, was erased through the Sacrament of Baptism and then that it was not. There was a hell; then there was not. There was a Purgatory and we should pray for the dead and then there was no help as we were all predetermined to enjoy eternal happiness in Heaven or condemned before birth to everlasting misery in hell.

Although he was tortured with self-doubts, tormented by thoughts that he might be leading the faithful astray, and if so what punishment awaited him from God the Father, Luther, because of the malignant growth of pride that had killed any and all semblance of the Augustinian monk who had once loved Mother Church, could not confess he might be in error and return to Mother Church who was waiting to embrace him warmly and welcome him back, celebrating the return of her prodigal son.[99]

Luther claimed that the Church had erred in Faith and Morals, in complete contradiction to St. Paul who said that the Church was the Pillar of Truth. But using this false accusation, maligning the Church founded by God the Son, Luther formed a church founded by man (himself) which would be followed by thousands upon tens of thousands of other churches being founded by other men.

Did you ever notice when one spouse is guilty of adultery, he/she uses every pretext to leave his or her spouse; instead of the wronged mate being vindictive, it is the guilty one who attacks viciously, maligning and doing all he/she can to undermine the other, and so it was with Luther. He attacked the Pope and the Church with the vilest language, commissioning an author and artist to create a blasphemous and completely disgusting caricatural portrayal of the Church and the Pope. This is hardly the expectations one would have of a leader of a religion. To think that this man, a sinner, could place himself above the Church founded by God, and dared to malign her in such a filthy and unfounded manner leads one to, out of mercy, pray for his immortal soul, not canonize him as some Luthers of today would do.

War and Peace and the struggle for the souls of the Faithful

Luther, as with all priests was ordained to preach the Gospel of Peace. [This is why when considering for entry into the Martyrology of the Church those who died for the Faith, no priest who bore arms is ever considered for the title of Martyr.] Luther preached to the peasants riling them up against the princes, inciting an already suffering people to turn themselves and Germany into a land of misery filled with darkness and devastation. No one and nothing was safe from his vile remarks, showing no respect for the Church he once belonged to, nor to the Mother of God who was once his Heavenly Mother, when he was a priest.

The princes and nobility had used Luther for all he was worth. They took advantage of his ravings to banish the Catholic Church in their principalities and steal the Papal lands in the bargain. They had been absolute rulers of the body; now they became little popes to rule the soul as well.

They accomplished two goals; they rid themselves of the need to follow any moral laws other than their own; (remember, Luther preached that every man was to live his life by his own set of morals) they made themselves richer by stealing what did not belong to them.

Even before his death in 1546, he had taken second place to the lunacy which he authored. It had gotten completely out of control. He could only watch it; he couldn't do anything about it. Californians who have seen brush fires can relate to the blaze which he began as an arsonist with a match in a dry forest. The blaze from that small match destroys thousands and tens of thousands of acres. So it was with Martin Luther. He sparked a flame which ignited all of Europe for a time. However, even before his death, it was dwindling, being extinguished by the loyal Catholics who would not accept his ravings.

It took one more man to rekindle that fire, which burned out of control, bringing about the ultimate loss of 6,000,000 Catholics. Luther's rebellion was on its way out until lust flamed the soul of another man, Henry VIII, King of England, Defender of the Faith, and the Tragedy of the Reformation continued.

Footnotes

[1] Mt 18:18

[2] Jn 17:20-23

[3] 1Jn 2:19

[4] *The Facts about Luther* - Msgr. Patrick O'Hare, LL.D

[5] his father's wishes for him

[6] Vedder-a non-Catholic writer

[7] bolded by authors as emphasis

[8] Hausrath-a non-Catholic writer

[9] Indulgence-remission of temporal punishment due for sins, and hence the satisfaction owed to God for one's sins is called an Indulgence. (Catholic Encyclopedia)

[10] His visit to Rome was *later used as* the cause of his disenchantment with the Church.

[11] In 1508, Luther had been made a professor of philosophy at the new Catholic University of Wittenburg.

[12]based on the opinions of a guide in Rome

[13]a book Protestant writers admit has some of the most objectionable language

[14]from his first biographer and pupil Mathesius (O'Hare p.59)

[15]*which remits all temporal punishment due for sins*

[16]*where, not all the temporal punishment is removed*

[17]Mt 18:18

[18]Catechism of the Catholic Church #1478

[19] Luther -*The Facts about Luther* - Msgr. Patrick O'Hare, LL.D.

[20]Jn 12:5

[21]because God wants all His children with Him in Heaven

[22]Luther -*The Facts about Luther* - Msgr. Patrick O'Hare, LL.D.

[23]Luther -*The Facts about Luther* - Msgr. Patrick O'Hare, LL.D.

[24]Part of Germany from where Luther came

[25]Luther -*The Facts about Luther* - Msgr. Patrick O'Hare, LL.D.

[26]Luther -*The Facts about Luther* - Msgr. Patrick O'Hare, LL.D.

[27]Luther -*The Facts about Luther* - Msgr. Patrick O'Hare, LL.D.

[28]Luther -*The Facts about Luther* - Msgr. Patrick O'Hare, LL.D.

[29]Luther -*The Facts about Luther* - Msgr. Patrick O'Hare, LL.D.

[30]Pope Leo X-*The Facts about Luther* - Msgr. Patrick O'Hare, LL.D.

[31]Luther -*The Facts about Luther* - Msgr. Patrick O'Hare, LL.D.

[32]Luther -*The Facts about Luther* - Msgr. Patrick O'Hare, LL.D.

[33]she had been a nun

[34]Luther -*The Facts about Luther* - Msgr. Patrick O'Hare, LL.D.

[35]by Luther's own admission

[36]Predestination - the determination beforehand, of someone's salvation (some are *predestined* to eternal damnation whereas others are *predestined* to be saved). Predestination, according to the Catholic Encyclopedia: *That God is selective, that he predetermines the eternal status of the souls of some individuals ahead of time was condemned by the Council of Mainz in 848.*

[37]Luther - *The Facts about Luther* - Msgr. Patrick O'Hare, LL.D.

[38]as he called his excessive mortifications

[39]Jas 2:14-23

[40]along with 7 books of the Old Testament, as well as removing certain words, and changing others to suit his new theology

[41]Jas 1:2

[42]Jas 1:6

[43]Jas 1:9

[44]Jas 1:12

[45]condemned, cursed

[46]Gal 1:8-9

[47]Father Ken Roberts during a Mission in Louisiana

[48] From the quotation by Archbishop Fulton J. Sheen *"Millions of favors*

are hanging from Heaven on silken cords - prayer is the sword that will cut them." - from *Lift up your heart - Our guide to Spiritual Peace* original publishers: McGraw Hill

[49]Mt 26:52

[50]At that time it was not a requirement that a Cardinal be exclusively an ordained priest or bishop.

[51]For more, read Bob & Penny Lord's chapter on the Renaissance in their book: *Scandal of the Cross and Its Triumph, Heresies throughout the History of the Church.*

[52]Illustrated World Encyclopedia, Bobley Publishing Co. Woodbury, N.Y. - 1967

[53]St. Augustine's *Confessions*

[54]a quotation from Protestant Professor Seeburg from Berlin who was no friend to the Catholic Church - Found in book: *The Facts about Luther* - Msgr. Patrick O'Hare, LL.D.

[55]impression

[56]plagiarism - to take the writings of another and pass them off as one's own

[57]quoting another Protestant historian *The Facts about Luther* - Msgr. Patrick O'Hare, LL.D.

[58]*The Facts about Luther* - Msgr. Patrick O'Hare, LL.D.

[59] paraphrased by the authors from reference from *The Facts about Luther* - Msgr. Patrick O'Hare, LL.D.

[60]Jn 13:34

[61]paraphrased by the authors

[62]Acts 9:4

[63]Holy Scripture reads: *"So faith by itself, if it has no works is dead."* Jas 2:17

[64]Phil 4:1

[65]*"I tell you, if they keep silent, the stones would cry out!"* Lk 19:40

[66]Mt 16:18

[67] especially in the Holy Eucharist Which is only in our Church

[68] a human founder of a new religion

[69]Mt 16:18

[70]condemned by Leo X

[71]Mk 9:29

[72]Mt 5:48

[73]spiritually reborn or as is heard today "born again"

[74] Luther - (Walch XIII 1480) *The Facts about Luther* - Msgr. Patrick O'Hare, LL.D.

[75]Luther

[76]Mt 22:37

[77]God's

[78]Mt 5:17

[79]Luther - from *The Facts about Luther* - Msgr. Patrick O'Hare, LL.D.
[80]those of the Catholic Church
[81] information derived from Luther himself in his work against *The Mass and the Ordination of Priests* - from the book: *The Facts about Luther* - Msgr. Patrick O'Hare, LL.D
[82]Jn 6:53
[83]Mt 18:6
[84]Mt 19:16
[85]saving
[86]Scripture alone
[87]Mt 11:29
[88]Rev 22:18
[89]Mk 9:47
[90]Ship, sailing vessel
[91]Mt 26:39
[92]Mk 3:25
[93]direct quotation from Luther - *The Facts about Luther* - Msgr. Patrick O'Hare, LL.D.
[94]direct quotation from Luther - *The Facts about Luther* - Msgr. Patrick O'Hare, LL.D.
[95]direct quotation from Luther - *The Facts about Luther* - Msgr. Patrick O'Hare, LL.D.
[96]direct quotation from Luther - *The Facts about Luther* - Msgr. Patrick O'Hare, LL.D.
[97]direct quotation from Luther
[98]direct quotation from Luther
[99]Lk 15:11-32

John Calvin

Father of Predestination

John Calvin

As we start each chapter, we have the desire to use the title *Beginning of the End*. Well, no chapter, no dissident deserves this more than Calvin and the long-ranging destruction he was able to bring about. He launched a campaign of division that would sweep Europe, the New World and finally the entire world. It was Calvin who ushered in the final blow to the Church in Europe. But the heretical teachings he initiated, although the basis of much that our separated brothers and sisters still believe, have become so splintered and fragmented, they are hardly accepted by those who owe their beginnings to Calvin.

We have said over and over again: *There is never revolution without a cause.* But it needs someone to bring the festering boil to a head. Problems were brewing below the surface; people were becoming more aware and consequently more dissatisfied with the lifestyles of their priests, failing often to see in them the Jesus Whom these *Ambassadors of Christ* were supposed to represent on earth. We often wondered why priests were killed along with heads of state, when a mad crowd revolted and the situation got out of hand. The clergy were closely associated with the royal houses and the wealthy, because one: many priests, bishops and cardinals came from these elite families, and two: even those who did not, had much land and power, acting more like princes than priests. All the people needed was for someone to bring to the forefront that which had been hidden in the deep recesses of their hearts. When the priests stopped bringing Jesus to the faithful, His helpless lambs became ready game for any hunter who ensnared them with *something* to believe in, no matter how heretical.

And so, the world was ripe for such as Calvin! The Church has always been and always will be *perfect*, as He Who is perfect founded her, but the sad truth is that the Church has often been in the hands of those who have strayed and ultimately failed Her. The reassuring truth is that Jesus, true to His Promise, has never allowed hell to prevail against His Church, and so the Church has lived on, with those who have left returning, and those who remained fighting for her, often at the cost of their lives and the lives of their loved ones. There is no other Faith in the world that can boast as many martyrs, as the Roman Catholic Church.

Who was John Calvin?

Luther was beginning his campaign to destroy all that the Church held dear, and with it the Church itself. The enemy, knowing that Luther would ultimately fail, was preparing the world for the one who would finish the job Luther had begun. Eight years before Luther was to place his 95 attacks on the Church, a baby was born. John Calvin was born into a successful well-to-do family in the north of France. He received the very best education, excelling in school - a truly brilliant student. But like so many gifted people, possibly not satisfied with all that God had bestowed upon him, he became involved with the *Religious Revolution* that had infiltrated the University. Revolution always seducing the young, appealing to their beautiful minds with *new ideas*, luring them to a new world built on sand, attracting them to a *new family* outside the Church they and their ancestors grew up in, they soon become fair game for any new preaching that tickles their ears. And because they are the cream of the crop, the future leaders of the world, they lead many, along with themselves, away from the Ship to Heaven, the Catholic Church.

Calvin's father, a successful lawyer whose practice was centered on the ecclesiastical courts,[1] was active in the workings of the Church; he and his family benefited handsomely from the rewards received both spiritually and financially because of his close association with the bishop and the Church. Calvin could not have attended his fine schools without the gainful compensations derived from his father's employment by the hierarchy of the Church. Although his father had high hopes for his son, praying he would use his gifts for the Lord and His Church, the sad truth was to be just the opposite. Calvin became attracted to Lutheran students who were infiltrating the University, and the forbidden literature they were disseminating to all the students. And so, Calvinism began with *disobedience!* Calvin, although seriously warned against reading such literature, as it could confuse and possibly lead him away from the Truth, ignored the ban, possibly (pridefully?) believing himself too strong, too bright to be suckered into that which he did not believe, and away from that which he did. Lucifer loves when we think we are too strong to succumb to temptation - the *We can handle it!* philosophy.

This flirting dangerously with religious concepts opposed to the Faith he was baptized into finally led Calvin out of the Church, it is believed around 1534. Was his first act of disobedience in defiance of all his father wanted for him? If so, how sad! Think of the destruction that can come about with one act of thoughtless pride. I remember the philosophy fed to our bright students in the 1960s - *"A little smoke of Marijuana won't hurt you."* developed into - *"Your life is your own!"* The result, a helpless victim falling deeply into the trap, insisting to himself, and then to loved ones, that what he does will only hurt him! Did the enemy fill you too, Calvin, with those false promises? Only God Who is the Judge of all knows. It is a lie in the Twentieth Century and it was no less a lie in Luther and Calvin's time. The ripple caused by the pitching of one little stone into a brook spreads until it spills into the rivers and possibly into the ocean, affecting the world.

Abandoning his studies, along with his education, and his Faith around 1534, Calvin began wandering about France preaching Lutheranism! He returned to Paris and joined other Lutherans distributing sacrilegious literature attacking the Mass, the Sacraments, and the many treasures of the Deposit of Faith. They posted them on all the buildings in Paris without regard to its holiness or un-holiness; churches, convents, homes, schools, town squares, nothing and no one was spared. The French became incensed at the outrageous slurs aimed at Mother Church, and filled with a fury that raged out of control, many of the dissenters were arrested and executed. Calvin barely escaped with his life, as he fled in the middle of the night.

He travelled to Switzerland, and in 1535 he began to write his book: *The Institutes.* He kept on adding to it, until it comprised four books filled with a most comprehensive understanding of Calvin's dreamt-up theology and a rigorous guide to organizing and running a Protestant church. The book has been lauded as having had the greatest influence on the spreading of Protestantism then and now. It was the instrument most used to influence those who were ready for a change, whether good or bad!

At twenty-seven years of age he was asked to speak in

the cathedral. This was the beginning of his career as *Prophet of Protestantism.* Geneva, where Calvin made his headquarters, was ripe for revolt. Out of a population of 13,000, only 1500 chose a council who would determine the fate of the masses. Although the battle initially was waged on a political battlefield, with the influx of the religious revolutionaries, it soon turned into a blood bath directed at Mother Church. Nothing was spared! As always they most viciously attacked our beloved Mass. Their offenses unchecked, they wantonly ran around destroying crucifixes,[2] smashing statues, stripping sacred paintings, breaking splendid stained glass windows showing the lives of Mary and the Saints. They demolished holy statues of Jesus, the Blessed Mother, the Angels and the Saints; paintings by the masters were ripped down and destroyed. When that was not possible because they were frescoes or adhered to the wall, they were painted over. It was one of the most vicious acts of Iconoclasm since it had been condemned centuries before.[3]

Statues of John Calvin and Jan Hus in Worms, Germany

In spite of the protests of the majority, the council passed a law prohibiting all the people held dear, beginning with the Mass. With the same blow, they elected to adopt the new doctrines of the agitators as the official teachings of the land. The majority were not united and consequently ineffective. The minority in charge bullied the people, insisting they obey the new ordinances and cease practicing their ancient Faith.

Ten weeks later, Calvin would venture into this climate

ripe for a prophet. He and his new-found friend, Farel[4] industriously went about instituting their new philosophy. But their holiday was to come to an abrupt halt when the secular powers that were in charge felt themselves losing ground; theses two might just take over the *governing branch* of the state. And so, Calvin and Farel were thrown out of Geneva in 1538. But as we have said, referring to the Soviet Union and the end of the Cold War, *The bear is not dead, only asleep*, so it was with Calvin and his cohort Farel. Three years later they resurfaced in Geneva. Calvin and Farel agreed the council would maintain full control over the secular government and they would be in charge of all matters referring to Religion and Morals.

Calvin and Farel kept the council at bay, as best they could; but the government never quite trusted them. This resulted in ongoing strife between them. But they never gave up. It took twelve years before Calvin was to realize his dream to make Switzerland a Protestant state. Although Calvin never held any political office, he was the power behind all the state officials. As they were in charge in name only, Calvin was the real power from 1553 until he died in 1564.

Calvin, using Luther's theology as his own, insisted that man was doomed before birth to be totally and irreversibly corrupt because of original sin, and consequently was incapable of doing anything good. As Calvin taught that the Sacraments had no salvific (saving) grace to wipe away sins, it would stand to reason, he would preach man was condemned irrevocably before he was born. What a cruel and unjust god he believed in, certainly not God the Father, He Who created us. Calvin's ability to draw anyone to his strange theology is beyond me. How can someone live in peace knowing that he is powerless to change the course of his life.

Calvin advocated *Justification by faith alone*, using Luther's distorted version of Holy Scripture[5] where he had added the word *alone*. This was also supposed to justify his theology that God created man *helpless* to participate in any way in his salvation - man having been created, by God the Father, without *free will*.

Sadly, as sins live on, errors live on! Luther planted the first seed of heretical belief in *Absolute Predestination*; but Calvin had to go one further. How else could he woo followers away from Luther! Calvin preached that some, *very few*, were created by God to enjoy eternal joy in Heaven. These were the specially chosen ones; they could do anything, commit unrepentant sins, and they would still go to Heaven. With equal *absolutism*, he insisted that there also were the multitudes, the many who were pre-chosen or predestined to suffer *eternal damnation*.

What reason did Calvin give for God pre-ordaining most of His children to a life of hopelessness, with nothing to look forward to but hell after death? What kind of Father would subject His children to this limitless torture, this unalterable cruelty? Why would our loving compassionate Lord condemn His beloved children to an irrevocable sentence of everlasting damnation? According to Calvin, most of God's creation, because they were born of a totally depraved corrupt human nature (through their first parents Adam and Eve), would suffer eternal punishment in hell, although through no fault of their own. Imagine this life of helplessness, no chance of pleading your cause to God, God stoically sticking to His preconceived plan of death eternal! How did Calvin explain Holy Scripture where Jesus said He came to do away with death? Why did Jesus die on the Cross - for just a few? Why would God, Who allowed His Son to die for the redemption of His children's sins, condemn them to hell?

Why? To quote Calvin, "He is a God of Justice." Is this why *few* Calvinists or Presbyterians[6] still believe this? But then if this important *central* dogma of Calvinism is no longer valid, and not worthy of obedience, are any of Calvin's doctrines valid? Dear God, did we lose millions of Catholics to something which no one believes in anymore?

Calvin insisted that this *Predestination* was a positive thing done by a *loving* God. How can preordained condemnation to hell be a loving, positive action? We ask how and then we ask how again? The answer is we are incredulous! But for over two hundred years Calvin's ministers preached and his followers believed in this no-way-out theology of doom. I could cry!

Since Calvin preached this lack of God's Mercy, it stood to reason he would eliminate all God's life-giving Sacraments of Mercy, of hope! Going beyond even Luther, Calvin rejected *all* the Sacraments, claiming no Heavenly Grace flowed through them. In an attempt to destroy the Catholic Church, Calvin and Luther not only rejected Jesus as the Cornerstone of the Church He founded, they tore His Church down by doing away with the Sacraments. So that he would not lose his followers when they discovered they were orphans,[7] Calvin used some of the Sacraments but solely as external signs of initiation. Sounds a little familiar: Do we not hear this used today in our Church: *Rites of Initiation* for *Baptism and Confirmation*? Make no mistake these are not external signs of initiation, but heavenly graces. We are joined or initiated into the Mystical Body of Christ, because these *Sacraments* are Gifts from God Himself that not only make us one, they confer grace upon us to complete the journey.

Till today, descendants of Calvinism believe that the Eucharist is only a symbol, and that the Mass is not the Sacrifice of the Mass - the ongoing Sacrifice of the Cross,[8] but strictly a memorial in commemoration of the Last Supper. Whereas Luther preached that there was the *temporary* presence of Jesus in the bread and wine, unchanged, remaining bread and wine,[9] Calvin vehemently rejected the Mass as a total deception, a counterfeit, a sham made up by man. Forgetting the Lord's words at the Last Supper completely, Calvin called the Holy Eucharist nothing but a symbol.

Wipe Jesus from the face of the earth and the world will forget He ever existed! The Saracens tried that and failed, because the souls of Catholics were so imprinted with their Savior that after hundreds of years of not being allowed to even hear the Name of Christ no less see His Image, they still worshiped Him in their hearts; and when they were once again allowed to practice their Faith, resume going to church and receive the Sacraments, they were ready - the Light that could not be hidden under the bushel basket shining again.

Calvin tried to wipe away every trace of the Catholic Church. He and his henchmen ran from Catholic Church to Catholic Church, on a wild rampage. They burned the priests' vestments; they threw out the altars containing the relics of Saints, replacing them with tables; they discarded the confessionals, labeling everything the faithful held dear for 1500 years as harmful idols.

Magnificent Cathedrals and parish churches glorifying the Lord, their warm splendor giving us a foretaste of the heavenly majesty we will behold when we reach the Kingdom, were replaced by cold, stripped churches focusing our attention horizontally on man rather than vertically on God. The fullness of the Sacrifice of the Mass, which reached its summit with the reception of the Resurrected Christ in Holy Communion, was now supplanted by Calvinist indoctrinated sermons[10] on Holy Scripture carefully worded to affirm Calvin's teachings and dispute the ancient traditions of the Catholic Church. The service included the recitation of prayers and the *symbolic* reception of Communion as a commemorative act of the Last Supper. If not for the congregation lifting their voices reverently in songs of thanksgiving, the service could hardly have been called a community at worship.

Each community was self-governed, independent of other communities. Its structure was comprised of pastors, deacons and elders, elected by the congregation. Till today, if the community does not agree with the pastor, he is asked to leave and is replaced by someone in agreement with their philosophy. This strictly democratic form has contributed to the watering down of many of the original doctrines of the founders, leading to the tens of thousands of denominations now existing among the separated brethren. The only sign of unity is at times visible when the different churches attend a synod called on a local or national level. The final findings are still dependent on the receptivity of the members of the individual churches.

Like Luther before him, Calvin held that only the Bible, that which is found in Holy Scripture, was to be obeyed. This is called *Sola Scriptura*, and it has survived till today among most Protestants. Calvin studied the Bible extensively, digging for the truth which he never found. Unlike so many former Protestant ministers who, upon carefully searching for the reason *not* to belong to the Catholic Church, found themselves more and more convicted that it was the only *true* Church,[11] Calvin wrote volumes of commentaries on the Bible, never recognizing the Lord Who was there pointing to the Church He founded. As Jesus said *"The Son of Man is before you and you recognize Him not."*[12]

The Reformed Church and the State are one

Calvin had two carefully formulated plans. First, he wrote *The Institutes of the Christian Religions* in which Calvin outlined *his* doctrines. Stressing the disciplines required to live a true Christian life, it also specified the morals a Christian should have, detailed the type of worship to be practiced, and lastly the way the churches were to be organized, of course under Calvin. This book was largely responsible for the spread of Calvinism throughout Europe.

Second, he went about forming the perfect society in Geneva, *his model city*, a city where the church (of course run by him) would be the power over the state. Although this did not sit well with the councils of the government, causing many serious conflicts, he soon was able to win them over to his way of thinking. In one breath the council was the *official word* as far as what doctrines would be taught, and then they passed a decree stating that *only* Calvin's *Institutes of the Christian Religions* was to be followed, under pain of death for those who disobeyed! Although the councils alone exercised the punishments and executions of those considered heretics, councilors (those who agreed solely with his *Institutes*) were all carefully chosen by Calvin.

Calvin, with his clever argumentation convinced many that he was God's prosecutor;[13] and he wielded his alleged God-given authority with a heavy hand, completely intolerant of any other theology, punishing those who disagreed with him. There was not a trace of religious freedom left; any form of the former belief in the Roman Catholic Faith was strictly prohibited. It was against the law to pray in Latin, no less attend Mass. To refuse to believe that the Pope was the antichrist or to dare to breath a word in his favor, no matter how small, could result in dire reprisals such as loss of property, jail or death as a heretic.

To keep his followers from regressing back to the

Catholic Church's teachings or possibly being contaminated by even Protestant doctrines other than his, all authors (whether or not they were known to be in favor of his new Reform Church) had to submit their writings to Calvin or his censors for careful scrutiny before their works could be published. It went to the extreme that every page had to bear two sets of initials, that of the author and that of the censor. Should any author disagree with the findings, insisting their manuscripts bore true teachings in keeping with the Bible, they were swiftly punished, many Protestant theologians, formerly in favor, being exiled with the promise of facing execution as heretics should they return. Anyone disagreeing with Calvin was considered a heretic, and could look forward to being tortured and ultimately beheaded.

Control was the word and it had no boundaries. Dancing was forbidden; only approved religious songs were permitted, eliminating all other music (especially any songs considered non-religious); dress codes of men and women were regulated with none excused from imprisonment for even the smallest infraction, no matter what their station in life was; even hair styles were to conform to this new puritanical way of life. To say Calvin ran a tight ship is not adequate to describe the rules he legislated; and this formerly undisciplined society not only loved it, they became his enforcers, reporting family and friends who were not adhering strictly to Calvin's ordinances.

Attendance at services was required five times a week. Infractions, such as failure to attend services at the prescribed times, to disagree with Calvin's sermons, to intimate he was not the best preacher and only authority on the Bible's teachings was serious, were all against the church and the state, and open to formidable punishment. These restrictions penetrated even the sanctity of one's home, with Calvin appointed ministers and elders going from house to house inspecting it for any contraband - pictures or statues of Mother Mary, the Saints, Jesus on the Cross, any Catholic prayer books and etc. They were equally intolerant of other Protestant religious beliefs and believers, such as Lutherans or Anabaptists, exiling them upon discovery. Calvin's teams carried a book containing the names of all the inhabitants of Geneva with comments next to their names: *How they had adhered in dress, in decorum, in attendance at service, in lifestyle.* They were judged and given marks based on degrees of piety, according to the standards of Calvin and his new world, to name a few comments: *lukewarm, devout, sinful.*

Neighbor began to spy on neighbor, reporting to Calvin's ministers the slightest transgressions.[14] Calvin was able to convince the citizens of Geneva that his way, this cold, puritanical, unloving way was the way of God and by practicing what he preached, they were living God's plan for them. They believed what he spoke and by living what they believed, they began to believe that they were the chosen people of God, they alone were God's people.

Former Catholic priests who had followed Luther now left him and joined Calvin. Dissident Lutherans, not satisfied, seeking new preaching, new ideas were captivated by the eloquent Calvin and joined him. With them, he staffed a new College dedicated to promulgating his new Reformed Theology. We find then, as today, that people want to be proud of what they believe in; they are not seeking a country club church. Then as now, they are willing to fight for what they believe, to live and die for what they believe. Calvin fired them up with his preaching, stern and demanding as it was, whereas many of their priests appeared to have grown soft and apathetic. And so they willingly joined Calvin's army, and attacking other Protestant religions as well as the Catholic Church, became the pivotal force in Protestantism spreading throughout the northern part of Europe swallowing up millions of Catholics, who not knowing their own Faith, followed this preacher who tickled their ears.

Not confident he could win the world with his theology, he formed armies of revolutionaries who went on wild rampages destroying churches, desecrating the Eucharist, smashing statues, stripping Catholics of all they once believed in. And if that did not ring the death knell on the Church, they tortured and killed priests, religious, and laity stubbornly faithful to the Church. Hate begets hate, anger begets anger, violence begets violence and so Catholics retaliated, brother killed brother and Jesus and His Mother Mary wept.

Thank God much of that which Calvin taught is not taught any longer. But his legacy included the rise of a madman, Oliver Cromwell of England, who followed his philosophy in a harsh form, called Puritanism. Cromwell murdered King Charles of England, tortured and killed any Englishman who did not accept his harsh rule and systematically set out to annihilate every Irish Catholic in the country.

He crushed an Irish uprising which lasted from 1641-1651, in which 600,000 Irish Catholic were massacred. Did anyone ever seriously believe that any of this was supposed to have been done in the name of Jesus?

Many of the lies Calvin created and then propagated about the Church have sadly lived on, with our brothers and sisters in Christ unaware they are not true. We pray that this Trilogy will in a small way enlighten those who have left Mother Church, and those who never knew her, to the *real truth*; and they will come back home to the Church Jesus founded, the Church which flowed from His most Sacred Heart on Calvary.

Footnotes

[1]courts within the Church determining matters of the Faith

[2]right from the time of Calvary, the enemy has not been able to bear Jesus on the Cross

[3]refer to chapter on Iconoclasm in Bob and Penny's book: *Scandal of the Cross and Its Triumph, Heresies throughout theHistory of the Church.*

[4]the primary agitator and proponent of Lutheranism

[5]Rom 3:28

[6]There is no longer a Religion called Calvinism; instead today they call themselves Presbyterian.

[7]Jesus said "I will not leave you orphans." He comes to us in the Holy Eucharist. Jn 14:18

[8]as we in the Catholic Church have always believed

[9]Whereas in contrast, we in the Catholic Church believe the consecrated Host is no longer bread but the *Body, Blood, Soul and Divinity of Christ*, and the contents of the chalice is no longer wine but the *Body, Blood, Soul and Divinity of Christ.*

[10]approved ahead of time by Calvin or those chosen by him

[11]and now as converts, attracting more and more ministers and their congregations to the Catholic Church

[12]Jn 14:9

[13]*The Catholic Church through the Ages* - Fr. Martin Harvey, S.J.

[14][God help us, it sounds like Hitler and his young elite who reported their own families, and felt proud they had done so then they saw them led away. They had been brain-washed into thinking they were doing this for the Fatherland and country came before God and family.]

King Henry VIII

King Henry VIII

Defender or Defector of the Faith?

What Luther could not accomplish, the enemy of Christ would use a King, *a Defender of the Faith*,[1] to bring about. Did King Henry VIII know what would be the final outcome of this one act of disobedience? If he had known that a chain reaction would occur that would cover all the innocent, unknowing faithful of Europe, would he have chosen flesh and power over his Church, would he have still said yes to sin and no to his Pope? Did he realize the price that would be paid by the children of his Realm, those he had pledged to protect?

As far back as the Fifth Century a battle has been going on in England between those who love Mother Church, and those who would destroy her. At that time, it was the *pagan* Jutes and Anglo-Saxons who were waging a cold-blooded, inhumane war against the faithful, their focus - to annihilate Catholics and all things Catholic in England. Catholics chose torture and death rather than worship the invaders' pagan gods.

In order to preserve and practice their Faith, a small remnant escaped to Wales and the Cornish mountains. A tiny catacomb church, made up of those who stayed, kept in touch with their Catholic family in Gaul (France), in an effort to keep their roots firmly planted in Rome, the seat of the Church. Hearing "the cry of the poor," Welsh Catholics came to England and evangelized to the pagan invaders. But the road was bumpy, and grew perilous with its dangerous curves. Instruction had to be done clandestinely because of the ferocious opposition by most of the Angles and Saxons who would have just as soon killed a Catholic as look at him.

This was the climate into which Pope Gregory the Great in the *Sixth Century*, chose to send thirty missionaries, accompanied by their rector St. Augustine of Canterbury, to evangelize the Anglo-Saxons. When St. Augustine and his monks arrived at the French side of the English Channel, they were warned to turn back because of the brutality of the Anglo-Saxons and the danger of crossing the Channel. But Pope Gregory had received word that there were Englishmen starving to hear the Word of God, and so he ordered Augustine and his missionaries on to England and possible martyrdom.

Unrest had been simmering in England, heresies running rampant behind the scenes, but dangerous nonetheless. The division which John Wycliff sowed in 1382, would ultimately become fuel for the fire ignited by another heretic - Jan Hus. Couple that with the pot that was boiling over through the seething discontent of super-intellectuals and *humanists*[2] in England and you have the beginning of the weakening and final erosion of the Catholic Church in England, in the Sixteenth Century.

The sad truth is that King Henry never wanted to split from the Church! In 1520, he wrote a paper[3] so powerfully affirming the Church's doctrine on the Sacraments and the everlasting *Supremacy* of the Papacy, he received the most highly treasured award from Pope Leo X - *Defender of the Faith*. It was a defense of Mother Church, in response to Martin Luther's 95 theses against Catholic teaching.[4] Even after Henry's defection, he would have put to death anyone in his kingdom advocating Lutheranism! When Henry's defense of the Church was delivered to the Holy See, the King's loyalty and reverence accompanied it, he expressed that his reason for writing his treatise was because *"Luther had declared war not only against Your Holiness but also against your office - against the See and the Rock established by God Himself."* Yet 15 years later, he would deal the blow that would accomplish that which Luther had failed to bring about - the demise of the Catholic Church in Northern Europe.

I could cry when I reflect on Luther and Henry, and other once-loyal sons of the Church who have gone astray. Until his final breath, Henry personally observed all the tenets of the Roman Catholic Church and insisted his entire Realm faithfully practice the Faith handed down by the Apostles. *He loved Mother Church!*

Catholic England was a nation envied by most other nations - her towering Cathedrals steeped in the finest Gothic architecture, her parish churches in even the smallest hamlet with spires reaching up to Heaven glorifying the Lord, all mutually paid for by gentry and commoner alike. Even the crowning of a new monarch was done in the Church, with the blessing of the Church, one of the Church's apostles officiating - the Church and the State celebrating as one, *in communion*, creating a splendid pageantry which the English highly treasured. The crown and the clergy working side-by-side, heresy was virtually unknown. But the common man was not aware that a storm was brewing in the horizon.

It all started when King Henry's brother Prince Arthur died and Henry married his widow, Catherine of Aragon. At first they were happy. Henry loved Catherine and she exercised great influence over him. He and Catherine had only one child, *a girl*, Mary. Catherine had had many miscarriages and was unable to have more children. This left King Henry without a male heir. Now, his claim to the throne was at best shaky. The throne had been gained by his family as *spoils of war* when in 1485, the Plantagenets lost the battle of Bosworth to his father King Henry the VII. The Plantagenets were regarded, by the people, as the only family with true *Royal* blood, and as such the only ones with the right to govern. As a Tudor, Henry was never quite accepted by his subjects.

Henry's father became the first *Tudor* King. Now, in the England of this period, the king was everything, the absolute ruler. The people of England have always loved, almost revered their royalty; but in the

Catherine of Aragon

Sixteenth Century the king was next to God! They considered him *divinely* chosen. Marriages in those days were arranged, more often than not, out of political expediency, especially in the case of royal houses of different nations uniting, strengthening their kingdoms through this liaison. His brother Arthur had married Catherine of Aragon to strengthen Spain and England as partners. Now King Henry VIII was being told that his right to the throne could possibly be in jeopardy *because* of his marriage to Catherine. Wanting to protect his position, King Henry followed the advice of some[5] within his court who advocated he marry Anne Boleyn, a lady of the Royal Court. Friends and relatives of Anne Boleyn made sure to remind him, lest he weaken, that her being from the Plantagenet family would help to insure his claim and that of his heirs to the throne of England. Some say, lust may have played a part in his decision-making, as he was a man who denied himself nothing - was known to be a glutton when it came to food and all forms of excess. But if so, it was not the *only* reason

Pope Clement VII

for his ultimate determination to have his marriage annulled.

Henry approached Pope Clement VII, petitioning him for an annulment of his marriage to the Queen. The King used the argument that his marriage to Catherine was invalid, as Pope Julius II was in error when he removed the encumbrance restricting him from marrying his dead brother's widow. Pope Clement VII would not agree to King Henry's annulment, insisting the special dispensation granted by the Pope was binding, because the marriage between his elder brother Prince Arthur and Catherine had never been consummated.

When the Pope refused to grant King Henry an annulment, a bishop - Stephen Gardiner went against his Pope and demanded Pope Clement grant Henry an annulment. A man of God and a Catholic, he had pledged to obey and defend his Pope above all others; yet he proffered his allegiance to his king, to the point of threatening the Pope with a schism. Now, *Bishop*

Anne Boleyn

Gardiner never really wanted to break from Rome. But when he made the decision to be more English than Catholic, siding with the King over the Pope, he was well on his way to paving the demise of Mother Church in England. The argument for the Supremacy of the Crown over the Church in England was: *The King is an Englishman; he knows us and our needs better than someone in Rome and he can better direct us in matters of the Faith. The Pope is not an Englishman with an Englishman's problems.*

[Sound familiar? Isn't that what a very vocal minority are saying, today: *How can someone in Rome understand the problems facing an American Catholic?* The first great error, and other errors follow once error begins and is not stopped, is the nomenclature or terminology that we are American Catholics. *We are no more American Catholics* than the English of Henry's day were *English Catholics*; we are *Roman* Catholics who are American. We are part of *One, Holy, Catholic, and Apostolic Church*, the *one* Universal Church, the same for *all people* dwelling in the four corners of the world. Jesus sent His Disciples to preach the good news to *everyone, the Good News*, not some good news, but *the Good News* as passed on from Jesus through His apostles. St. Paul said, we were no longer Gentile or Jew but brothers and sisters with *One* Father and *One* Lord Jesus Christ.]

Stephen Gardiner and Englishmen of his day all believed that the abyss that had developed between the King and the Pope was just another argument, the chasm that separated them was only temporary and would close. They were sure it would soon

Stephen Gardiner

blow over. Were they aware that by going along with the King they were *disobeying* the universal *God-given* authority of the Pope? Their argument was that the King was a loyal Catholic; the Pope himself declared Henry *Defender of the Faith*. Why could the Pope not grant him this one small favor! Surely the Pope would use the loop hole presented to him to get out of this sticky situation.

In any event, they put the king of this world[6] above *the* King of all eternity, our Lord Jesus Christ, because as Saint Catherine of Siena said, our Pope is *"Sweet Christ on earth."* Little did they foresee the threat to all they believed and held dear. Because make no mistake about it, not even King Henry the VIII would have knowingly broken one tiny particle of the Doctrine of our Church. How were Stephen Gardiner and the average Englishman of that day to know that disobedience, on what they judged a small matter, would slowly but surely separate them from the Church that Jesus Christ Himself founded, and with the Church, the Mass and the Sacraments as they knew them.

[Did Eve argue with Adam that eating of the Tree of Knowledge was a small matter? We know what that *one act* of disobedience led to. As you travel with us through this very sad part of our history, ask yourself why our Lord has guided you to read this book. Are we not hearing today, false prophets promoting: *"You can be a good Catholic without the Pope."*]

Now Stephen Gardiner *and* King Henry the VIII were deeply Catholic, not only in Doctrine but in full practice. They upheld and defended all the ancient traditions of the Church which included the Mass, with the full doctrine of the Real Presence of Jesus in the Eucharist, *Body, Blood, Soul and Divinity* not only at the moment of consecration but as long as He was present - at Mass, in the Tabernacle, or in a Monstrance; they continued to propagate *all* the tenets and devotions of the Faith. But one act of disobedience leads to another. The message went out loud and clear. The bishops and the men around Henry thought if they were above the authority of the Pope who came from sixteen centuries of unbroken succession of the Papacy,[7] then why not question the *Real Presence of Jesus in the Eucharist*, why not challenge and change all that had been passed down to them, that they had believed in for 1600 years? But they dared not act openly until Henry died!

Now Henry was not beneath having affairs, but when he approached Anne Boleyn,[8] she was not about to give into his *physical* demands without marriage. Nevertheless, she moved into his royal apartment in September 1532 and began secretly living with Henry; by Christmas, she was expecting a child. She exerted relentless, never-ending pressure on him to have his marriage annulled. Tired of hearing her carping, Henry began his adamant quest to have his marriage to Catherine set aside. He went round and round with the Pope for six years! Desperate and completely dominated by Anne Boleyn, now that she was with child,[9] Henry threatened the Pope! He even tried to coerce him into bending to his will using the veiled threat that Rome could lose England.

When all his maneuvering failed, he concentrated on his bishops and clergy. Henry called them to meet with him, with the express purpose to approve a document acknowledging him as *"The Supreme Head of the Church and the clergy of England."* His Primate - Cardinal Warham of Canterbury agreed, but with one restriction: He insisted that the following be added: *"as far as the law of Christ allows."* July, 1533, Pope Clement excommunicated Henry! That sentence was later reversed only to be re-instated by the Pope to follow Pope Clement.

Upon the death of Cardinal Warham, King Henry

appointed *Thomas Cranmer*,[10] as the *new* Primate. Soon after, King Henry secretly married Anne Boleyn. Four months barely passed when Cranmer, now *Archbishop Cranmer* nullified Henry's marriage to Catherine of Aragon and declared the King's marriage to Anne Boleyn legal. This came to pass in 1534.

Upon hearing this, the Pope solemnly declared Henry's marriage to Catherine of Aragon *binding* and that of Anne Boleyn as *null and void*! But laws were already being formulated and passed in England in March, prior to the Pope's edict, placing all members of the clergy under the Crown, as well as all properties, financial assets and etc. Things began to escalate dangerously. September 25, 1534 Pope Clement VII died and Paul III was elected Pope. November of that year the English Parliament passed the formal *Act of Supremacy*:

"Be it enacted by the authority of this present parliament, that the king, our sovereign lord, his heirs and successors, kings of this Realm, shall be taken, accepted and reputed the only supreme head on earth of the Church of England called Anglicana Ecclesia."[11]

This declaration encompassed all matters of Church originally under the supreme authority of the Pope as Head of the Church. With this document, Henry the VIII was declared the *final word* on all matters of faith and worship. The king exacted from all his bishops and priests total and uncompromising obedience to him as Supreme Head of the Church. Then Henry issued a formal edict denouncing Pope Paul III!

All but one of Henry's bishops went along with Henry. That bishop, *St. John Fisher*, paid for his loyalty to Jesus and His Pope, by undergoing a horrible Martyr's death.[12] Although these bishops deserted the Ship of the Church, the laity did not. The great love and faithfulness the people of

England had for Mother Church was manifested by rivers of blood flowing from thousands and thousands of martyrs who chose death rather than renounce their Faith and their Pope. Henry's trusted friend and chancellor - *St. Thomas More* would not go along with Henry and his puppets - anti-Catholic bishops, and suffered the same fate as St. John Fisher; he was beheaded!

St. Thomas More

Pope Paul III called a council to reform the Church and chose two delegates from England to participate. Henry

St. John Fisher

had one delegate killed and had the 80 year old mother of the second killed because he could not get his hands on him, as he had already left England. Although it has been believed that the Pope had Henry excommunicated because he had declared himself Head of the Church of England, we discovered in our research[13] that Pope Paul III not only excommunicated Henry, but placed the whole of England under an interdict[14] because of this final heinous act.[15]

The evil that man does lives after him

Henry by this time was deeply aligned with the nobility and their agenda, and was further weakened by the venereal disease that was taking over his body and mind. He could not have foreseen the catastrophic consequences of his disobedience and misplaced pride. The whole idea had never been to bring about a schism, at least not on Henry's part. It did not begin that way; it was not Henry's plan, nor his aim, to break irreconcilably with the Pope; but break he did and schism did come about.

Although he believed there was no recourse but to disobey the Pope, King Henry went about making sure that none of the Dogmas or Tenets of the Faith would be sacrificed in the process. It was not Henry's intention to *change* the Church in England, to alter its Catholicity with an influx of Protestantism; but nevertheless Lutheran and Calvinist ideas were clandestinely infiltrating the country; and like it or not, England would be the instrument to deal a death blow to Catholicism and give new life to Protestantism. Forces in England would not only resuscitate, but *fortify* a heretofore dying Lutheran and Calvinist movement in the rest of Europe. Luther - a *priest*, King Henry - a *Defender of the Faith*, and Calvin - a dedicated *layman* were all good men who went astray; but as with the many who preceded and followed them, the repercussions were nonetheless disastrous.

Whereas Henry became more stubbornly Catholic in his defense of the Church's Dogmas, his bishops became more and more *anti*-Catholic, inch by inch clandestinely changing, aborting, and ultimately throwing out all the Treasures of the Roman Catholic Church in England, in exchange for favors granted by the privileged class who benefited from the split with Rome.

As long as King Henry the VIII was alive, priests and

bishops were *compelled* to faithfully pass down all the doctrines and practices of the Roman Catholic Church, under pain of death. But soon after King Henry VIII died, those who were left went about with their plans to destroy the Faith and its teachings, in England. Henry's heir to the Throne was his *diseased* son Edward by his third wife Jane Seymour who succeeded Anne Boleyn as Henry's Queen, after Henry became disenchanted with Anne, and had her beheaded.[16] Now

Jane Seymour

Edward was no match for these bishops and wealthy land-owners. Weakened by the blood of his father who already was suffering from venereal disease, a product of his many indiscretions, Edward reigned in *name only*.

Henry had possibly foreseen the attacks that would befall his kingdom after his demise. In 1539, he had brought pressure to bear on parliament to pass the *Six Articles* he had drafted. As Defender of the Faith, he had defended his Church and her Sacraments against Luther. He never ceased believing it was his *Divine* responsibility *to* protect *the Church in England*. This edict clearly defended

- the Dogma of *Transubstantiation*,[17]
- *Communion* under one Specie,
- *Masses for the dead*,
- *The Sacrament of Penance* (or Confession),
- the taking of *vows* such as poverty, chastity and obedience

Archbishop Thomas Cranmer

- and as is required of all religious - the vow of celibacy.

After Henry's death Edward VI was betrayed by his own uncle - the Duke of Somerset who made himself *Lord Protector* of England, and by Archbishop Cranmer who was subsequently rewarded for his part in the treachery by being placed in charge of the Church and altering her dogmas. Cranmer began by ordering Parliament to rescind King Henry's *Six Articles*. In addition, he had them reverse the laws against heresy. Protestant preachers were imported to teach and preach a Church more Lutheran and Calvinist than Catholic. And they did it all in the name of King Edward VI who was merely a helpless puppet in their hands.

The Book of Common Prayer was drafted by Archbishop Cranmer in which he instituted *his own ideas*. The greatest single attack was condemnation of the Sacrifice of the Mass, the new heretics calling it *idolatrous*. They removed all mention in *their new services* of the priest as *victim-priest*; who was made to resemble more and more Calvinist preachers who were riding herd over the Church in England. Well they had to do that, as they were demeaning the *Sacrifice* of the Mass. In this way they could do away with the Cross - Easter people without Good Friday. If Henry were in Purgatory, his greatest pain had to be witnessing the Church he had held dear being destroyed.

When the second edition of *The Book of Common*

Prayer was released it did away with the last vestige of belief in the Sacrifice of the Mass, and belief in the True Presence of Jesus in the Blessed Sacrament became a *crime* punishable by death. Bishops who clung to the teachings of the Church, regarding the Mass and the Sacrament of the Eucharist were either imprisoned and tortured, or at best relieved of their dioceses. Altars of Sacrifice were removed from the sanctuary; they were replaced by *"decent tables"*[18] which were then placed in the *midst* of the congregation. The lesson, loud and clear, was that this was not a Sacrifice but rather a *symbolic* remembrance of the Last Supper.

[Does this sound familiar - with the alterations that are being made today, stripping, modernizing and refashioning our beautiful Catholic churches into buildings resembling cold gymnasiums, and all in the name of complying to a code?[19] Does this not smack of the changes forced upon the faithful in England 500 years ago? Is Jesus asking: Who will choose Me this time, instead of Barabbas?]

Part of the necessary changes included bishops and priests taking Relics of Saints and Martyrs which had reverently been inserted in the Altars, and disdainfully tossing them in the vestibules of the churches. As the faithful had to pass this way to enter the church, they required the faithful show *their* contempt for the Reality of the Sacrifice of the Mass by stomping and crushing the Relics underfoot. In addition, the faithful helplessly stood by, as they threw out the Altars upon which Mass had been celebrated for hundreds of years, and smashed them to bits, sounding the message loud and clear: *The Mass is no more!*

But not all went along with Cranmer. Many gave their lives, rather than deny their Lord and Savior - the One Who went to the Cross for them, the One Who kept His promise and remained with them in the Blessed Sacrament. It was through their sacrifice, their martyrdom, their unity with the

Victim-Priest that a tiny remnant had the zeal and courage to remain faithful to the Catholic Church. It was from these brothers and sisters that others drew their strength to go on believing in the One, Holy, Catholic, Apostolic Church of their ancestors. Holding up through persecutions upon persecutions lasting hundreds of years, they became an underground Church, a catacomb Church. Many suffered a dry martyrdom.[20] It is because of their love and courage, their martyrdom, their undying faith in the Church founded by Jesus Himself that whole parishes of Anglican brothers and sisters, along with their pastors, are returning Home to Mother Church.

There has always been struggle between the majority who love the Church and the powerful few who want to destroy her for their own personal gain. As reconciliation with the Pope would mean giving up much of the wealth they had accrued by unprincipled confiscation of land and property (from the Church), those who were in power were for an all out break with the Church. *Now* Stephen Gardiner came out strongly against their proposed schism, arguing it would lead to the final death of the Magisterium in the Church of England.

Considering Stephen a dangerous adversary, the landowners, along with the bishops, imprisoned him in the Tower of London and took away his faculties as bishop. The physical torture he had to endure did not compare to the anguish he suffered beholding the fruits of his disobedience - the demise of his Church. He had unknowingly been an instrument of the enemies of the Church. Now a victim to the monsters he had unwittingly given birth to, he had to stand helplessly by and watch them force a new religion upon his fellow Englishman, in many cases, violently. Oh how the average Englishman longed to return to the days under the Pope.

After six short years, the tiny, frail and sickly King Edward died. And by virtue of King Henry's will, Edward's half-sister Mary Tudor, daughter of Henry and Catherine of Aragon, succeeded him to the throne. The English received their new Queen with open arms, as she represented the return of their Roman Catholic Faith. One of her first acts was to have Stephen Gardiner released from the Tower of London, and bestow upon him the greatest responsibility and highest position in England that of Chancellor.[21] He did not use his office and position to bring about personal gain, nor did he exercise his duties with political motives in mind. Rather, his focus was to bring back to England that which she had lost.

His punishment, greater than that in the Tower was to awaken to the nightmare before him - an anti-Catholic governing body, the total suppression and ultimate banning of the Mass, the wanton razing of churches and altars. The hostility reached such a feverish pitch, there was rampant, senseless demolishing of everything reminiscent of the Catholic Church: they ripped down crucifixes and smashed statues of Jesus, Mother Mary, the Angels and the Saints; they even desecrated the incorrupt bodies of Saints and then burned them beyond recognition; they plundered and ravaged Shrines to our Lady and the Saints.

If like St. Paul, Stephen Gardiner had been zealous in his persecution of the Church, he now used all that zeal to try to repair the damage he had done. As he walked through the holocaust brought about by disunity, he became more and more determined that unity with the Papacy was the only way. He spent the rest of his life trying to undo the harm he had caused. The Lord gave him only two years to bring back to the faithful that which had been taken from them - their beloved Church. Before he closed his eyes for the last time, he did see the victory of a united Church in communion with the Pope and Rome. Thank God, he mercifully died before its demise.

"I denied as Peter did, I went out as Peter did, but I have not wept as Peter did." These were the dying words of Stephen Gardiner, a penitent who had not only believed in the Supremacy of the King in matters of the Church in England but at one point, actually threatened Pope Clement with *schism* if he did not grant King Henry his annulment.

"I denied as Peter did." Gardiner equated his disobedience to the Pope, our *Sweet Christ on Earth,*[22] with Peter's denial of the Lord on the Way of the Cross.

"I went out as Peter did." After he saw the havoc and utter destruction of all he believed, Gardiner repented denying the authority of the Lord's vicar and spent his last years uniting the Church in England to her Pope whose loss the faithful of England so deeply mourned. Peter spent the rest of *his* life repenting *his* denial of Jesus and went about preaching, in spite of threats by the Sanhedrin, until at his final moment, feeling totally unworthy to die as His Savior before him, he requested he be crucified upside down.

"...but I have not wept as Peter did." It is said that Saint Peter wept so passionately because he denied Jesus three times, the tears running down his face formed deep ruts. As Peter before him, Stephen Gardiner never forgot his betrayal of the trust placed in him by Jesus his Lord. He grieved until he saw the return of the Church to his fellow Englishmen. Our Lord was merciful in that Gardiner was spared witnessing the far-reaching dissemination of everything Catholic that came about after Queen Mary's death three short years after his own death.

This one act which started on an island[23] was to result in its tentacles crossing the channel to the continent - spreading Protestantism in the rest of Europe. As the old saying goes, especially true in this case, *"As England goes, so goes the world."* The evil that man does lives long after he is gone.

Five years of Heaven and forty-six years of hell

Queen Mary, upon succeeding her half-brother Edward, immediately restored the Faith to the people. Bishops who had been relieved of their dioceses were called back. She vowed to return the church in England to her rightful place, under the Chair of Peter, and she went about it with a tireless zeal, cleaning house, so to speak, where it had to be done. Those who had instigated the takeover of Protestantism in England were exiled!

Naturally she would next turn to Archbishop Cranmer. During Edward's reign, Archbishop Cranmer had been *the* driving force behind the *persecution* of Catholics who remained faithful to the Church and her Pope, and as he had not only been the primary *author* but *implementer and enforcer* of Calvinist and Lutheran services that had replaced the Sacrifice of the Mass, when Mary ascended the throne, he knew he was in trouble. At first, to save his life he asked pardon of the new Regent. But he did not have a conversion of heart; he went about telling some within the court *privately* that he was just being expedient and *denied* disdainfully that he had ever, nor would he ever celebrate Mass for the Catholic Queen. Egged on by those who were deriding him and mocking him for his cowardly defection from that which he truly believed,[24] he wrote down his personal and most private feelings toward the Catholic Church; but at the last moment he was too frightened to make it public. There were those who for whatever reason, had it printed. When it reached the Crown, he was brought before the royal magistrates and tried for heresy!

Part of the serious charges against him were: He had not only done all in his power to do away with the Holy

Mass, but he had instituted laws making the reception of the Sacrament of the Eucharist a *crime punishable by death.* He was found guilty and relieved of his position. Now, although the execution of an Archbishop was something unheard of, realizing how passionate were feelings against him for the brutal betrayal of his flock,[25] and believing death was imminent unless he repent, Cranmer threw himself on the mercy of the Crown. He implored the Queen not to impose this sentence on him as he was an Apostle of Christ. Using great remorse, calling himself a worthless sinner unworthy of her forgiveness and likening himself to the good thief beside Jesus who was truly sorry for his sins, he wrote that he knew it could only be by Jesus Himself and through His Mercy that he could be absolved of his heinous crime, especially that which led so many unsuspecting lambs astray.

Insecure, and fearing at times that his remonstrations had not successfully deceived the Crown, he continued protesting he was truly sorry. On the day that had been set for his execution, he was brought to the Church of St. Mary in Oxford where a priest was to preach on the situation; then Cranmer was to publicly renounce all that he had advocated during the reign of Edward VI and ask for pardon. As publicly disavowing heresy always meant a reprieve, Cranmer prepared his speech beforehand, with this in mind. But all his high hopes were soon lost when the priest announced the decision had been passed down: *He was to be punished as a heretic.* Cranmer ascended the altar bringing his written statement with him; but judging it was all hopeless, he now recanted all he had formerly said and insisted it had been merely to save his life. He proclaimed that he not only did *not* consider the Pope the rightful Supreme Head of the Church, he did not consider the Catholic Church the true Church and did not believe in anything it teaches.

Then Cranmer darted out into the pouring rain, the mob in hot pursuit. When they closed in on him, they tied him to a stake and burned him as a heretic. As the fire was rising, consuming his body, he raised his right hand in disdain and thrust it into the fire, fulfilling what he had said he would do upon death: retract all he had written admitting his errors.

Under the law, at that time, once someone was condemned as a heretic and turned over to the government, the sentence was never commuted.[26] But had he at the last moment, even at the stake, showed that his loyalty to the Church and subsequently the Crown was not merely to escape death, we have to wonder if he would not have been released? After all, there had been cases where this had happened. Had he acted too hastily at the church, or at the stake? Only Cranmer and the God of Justice know. But there is a sadness; this man of God who had been entrusted with so much, had fallen so low. God have mercy on his soul. It was because of this and similar incidents that Queen Mary was donned *"Bloody Mary"* by Protestant writers and historians. Not having lived at that time and in those circumstances, we make no judgment on either side.

England was once again in total communion with the Pope. He was reinstated Supreme Head of the Roman Catholic Church in England. Priests and bishops loyal to the Church dispensed the Sacraments once more. Churches were filled to capacity! All England rejoiced; but their joy turned to sadness. Queen Mary died, and the Catholic Church in England died with her.

The crown passed to Elizabeth. The poor people of England believed their new queen, when she professed her undying loyalty to the Roman Catholic Church and vowed to defend her. And so, *once again* they rejoiced! And once again, their rejoicing turned to mourning. Unlike her half-sister Mary who reigned only five years, Elizabeth and her aide-de-camp Lord Cecil would wage a *Reign of Terror* against Catholics in England which would last forty-six years, the blood of innocents flowing through the streets. The majority, more out of fear than allegiance, followed the queen. But that tiny remnant that kept the Church alive in England, wholeheartedly gave their lives for the Faith. They willingly suffered torture on the rack. They professed their Faith right up to the moment the noose tightened around their necks choking out their last words of love for Mother Church. Many cried out with their Lord, *"Forgive them they know not what they do,"* as they placed their heads on the block, facing death by the axe.

The death of the Catholic Church in England was due largely to the greed of the nobility, the *few* who insisted on holding onto that which was never rightfully theirs. Although they had illegally obtained their lands from the Church, when one lives a lie long enough the lie becomes the truth; they would not relinquish to the Church that which belonged to her. As reconciliation would mean just that, of course they were opposed.

Elizabeth was a willing partner of the wealthy, not only unfaithful to her loyal subjects who trusted her, but *faithless* to the Church King Henry had vowed to defend, completely disregarding her dead father's wishes.

The Parliament in 1559, reinstated the Oath of Supremacy, only it was changed to read *"the Queen's Majesty"* has the supreme power over all Ecclesiastical and Civil matters of the Realm. Elizabeth refused to be called, like her father, *"Vicar of Christ and Supreme Head of the Church."* The Oath passed a law forbidding the celebration of, and participation in the Sacrifice of the Mass. It demanded that all the faithful adhere *solely* to the new prayers dictated by the Crown (now largely influenced by Lutherans and Calvinists), along with discarding and discontinuing the use of all former Catholic prayers and Sacraments passed down by the Catholic Church. To disobey brought a penalty of death. Differing from the position taken under King Henry, who had preserved all the Dogmas and Tenets of the Catholic Faith with the exception of allegiance to the Pope, this was now a large scale attempt to kill the Church in England.

All the bishops with one exception, condemned these statues and refused to comply. They were either imprisoned, forced to relinquish their dioceses, or were exiled. Originally the priests followed their bishops' leads, and remained faithful to Mother Church. But then the god of security lured them into disobeying their bishops, leading them to betray the vows they had taken on the day of their ordination, the bait - the Crown's promise they would keep their parishes and the income derived from them, if they took the Oath. Half the priests capitulated and took the Oath of Supremacy. Masses were outlawed, and *at first* to attend or celebrate Mass would cost a heavy fine, the seizing of assets, and/or imprisonment. Later the penalty would escalate to a death sentence.

Enter Mary Queen of Scots! Mary Stuart,[27] fearing her life was in danger, asked her cousin Elizabeth for asylum from the Calvinists who had taken control of Scotland, and Elizabeth said yes. When Queen Mary first arrived in England all went well, until Lord Cecil[28] concocted an alleged plot by

Mary, Queen of Scots

Queen Mary to overthrow Queen Elizabeth and take her place as Regent of England. Queen Elizabeth went along

Queen Elizabeth I

with Lord Cecil, although she was not comfortable with imprisoning a member of the Royal Family, and not really convinced of Mary's guilt. But as she was more fearful of this walking time bomb; she had seen what happened if he was crossed; and what if he were right! Elizabeth betrayed the trust Mary Stuart had placed in her and placed her in prison.

Now, it just happened to be that many Englishmen considered Queen Mary Stuart the rightful heir to the throne, as she was the *legitimate* child of Queen Margaret, daughter of Henry VII, whereas Elizabeth was the *illegitimate* offspring of Henry's invalid marriage to Anne Boleyn (made invalid and bigamous because he was still married to Catherine of Aragon when Elizabeth was conceived). Fear taking over reason, Elizabeth had Mary Stuart dragged from dungeon to dungeon over a period of twenty years, and finally had her put to death.

Queen Elizabeth was excommunicated by Pope Saint Pius V! This brought about a wave of terror against Catholics that resulted in them being executed as traitors. Although it was not meant to give rise to Martyrs, it did; and those Martyrs gave the few who held on, the strength and courage to stay faithful. This systematic *ethnic cleansing*[29] of Catholics and the Catholic Church resulted in future generations knowing little about the Faith of their ancestors. Only a remnant remained.

By 1606 England was in chains, as she became more and more immersed in the cruelty, the all-encompassing, sweeping wave of persecution that comprised the furor of penal times. There was not a monastery, convent or shrine to be found. To celebrate or to attend Mass, to convert to the Catholic Church or to be a party to someone else's conversion[30] would result in a death sentence. In order to hold any position of trust or importance, whether small or large, one was required to recognize the successor of *Henry VIII* as head of the Church in England, not the successor of *St. Peter*, our first Pope. If that was not bad enough, it was compulsory for Catholics to not only attend Protestant services, but to receive communion there. To not do so, was to face a charge of treason which carried a penalty of imprisonment and death. Many fled to the continent of Europe rather than be party to such a serious blasphemy, and some stayed in spite of the ongoing tyranny. Brave and dedicated missionaries, especially Jesuits, stood by them, strengthening them, giving them much needed support.

Now for a Roman Catholic to receive Communion in a Church other than in a Catholic Church, from a priest or minister who has not the faculties to consecrate the host into Holy Communion, is to be party to creating a scandal on the Catholic Church and guilty of breaking the Eighth Commandment - *"Thou shall not bear false witness"* for when we receive in our Church we are declaring along with our Profession of Faith that we are in communion with the entire Church and all she teaches. The Holy See in the following excerpt from the Catechism of the Catholic Church explains it thusly:

"...the Apostle has to exhort Christians to `maintain the unity of the Spirit in the bond of peace.' What are these bonds of unity? Above all, charity `binds everything together in perfect harmony.' But the unity of the pilgrim Church is also assured by <u>*visible bonds*</u>[31] *of communion:*

-profession of one faith;

-common celebration of divine worship, especially of the Sacraments;

-apostolic succession through the Sacrament of Holy Orders, maintaining the fraternal concord of God's family."[32]

The Catechism of the Catholic Church goes on to state:
"Sacrilege is a grave sin especially when committed against the Eucharist, for in this Sacrament the true Body of Christ is made substantially present to us."[33]

In the Catechism we also find this truth that has transcended time and endless persecution:
"By the consecration the transubstantiation of the bread and wine into the Body and Blood of Christ is brought about. Under the consecrated species of bread and wine Christ Himself, living and glorious, is present in a true, real, and substantial manner: His Body and His Blood, with His Soul and Divinity (cf. Council of Trent: DS 1640; 1651).[34]

Should a Catholic knowingly receive communion in a non - Catholic Church, he is either stating:

-that he does not believe in that which the Catholic Church most emphatically teaches - Our Lord is truly present Body, Blood, Soul and Divinity after the consecration of the bread and wine,

-or that in this non-catholic Church they have the same Sacraments we have,

-that its members obey the successor of Peter,

-and they believe as we do in *all* the Tenets of our Catholic Faith.

We have to pause and ask ourselves how brother could act against brother and sister against sister, inflicting this no-win kind of sentence upon those they love. They were damned if they did and damned if they didn't. Whether they believed or not, how could anyone subject someone who *does believe* to choosing between either death of the body or death of the soul? If they refused to abide by the demands passed down by the authorities, they could count on losing two thirds of their property; they could not have highly respected professions such as doctors or lawyers; they were barred from serving in the armed forces; they could not further their education by attending the universities, and if in desperation families sent their children abroad to receive their education, their inheritance was forfeited and turned over to other members of the family who were Protestant.

In a land where at one time you could see women fingering rosaries, attending Mass every day, praying many *Our Fathers* in public, reading aloud the Office of our Lady in church, twenty years later, all was gone. Nowhere was a Crucifix to be found; gone were all the statues of Mother Mary; and if someone was caught with a Crucifix or statue of Mother Mary, the Angels or the Saints, the family was insulted and degraded in the town square, their crucifixes and statues were mocked and horribly profaned, and more often than not, their homes were confiscated. And all as punishment because they dared to be Catholic in their own homes. Justices of the Peace were given unrestrained rights to search and ransack homes and places of business at will. No one was safe. The hounds were out and their bite was swift and deadly. The lesson came forth loud and clear: The Crown was your god - obey! To be very honest, historians will admit that there were no theological differences at the root of this division, but instead craven lust of property and power.

If it had been up to the faithful of England, who never stopped loving Mother Church, the abbeys would have returned, the convents and monasteries restored to the religious who had built and occupied them for centuries. But that would have meant landowners returning that which they had stolen; and as so often happens when with the passing of time - deceit becomes decree, theft becomes title. Wailing could be heard throughout the land - Rachel crying for her children, only it was Mother Mary.

"A cry was heard at Ramah

sobbing and loud lamentation:
Rachel bewailing her children
no comfort for her, since they are no more. "[35]

Mother Church, great mother that she is, always sends help to her children, in response to Jesus' promise that not a hair would be touched on the heads of His children and hell would not prevail against His Church. From the very beginning of the Church, whenever the innocent lambs of God were being attacked by wolves, the Lord raised up powerful men and women to defend His flock.

It was the Sixteenth Century and England was again in crisis. Their families had lived through that dark period in England,[36] centuries before under invaders, when bells no longer rang out calling people to worship. England in the Sixteenth Century was seeing history repeating itself; the days of Martyrs and Martyrdom was upon the British Isles once again, with multitudes of English Catholics being slaughtered, choosing death rather than deny their Faith. Once again, they were called to shed their blood rather than betray the Church and deny Christ's vicar as head of the Church, and they said yes! The enemy killed everyone, regardless of age, whom they suspected of being Catholic, but they could not kill the Church.

In the Sixth Century, St. Augustine of Canterbury restored ancient churches destroyed by the Anglo-Saxons, as he and his monks restored Catholicism to the English people. In the Sixteenth century there was a new invasion against Mother Church, once again the destruction and stripping of churches in an endeavor to wipe Catholicism out of the hearts of the English Catholics. But the Church refused to die. The Church in Rome once again saw her children suffering and she responded! She sent priests to save her children. Her *Ambassadors of Christ*[37] said *yes*, knowing it would result in the loss of their lives. Is this why the Anglicans are returning by the tens of thousands to Mother Church? It has always been the only way, through the shedding of blood, Martyrs' blood that the Church continues to rise again and again! It is on this martyrdom that the Church is rising once again, our precious English brothers and sisters coming back Home. The Martyrology of the Catholic Church in England could fill volumes.

Evil was not meant to be born into the world; it is the result of good being contaminated that brings evil into the world. God gives us a chance, new beginnings with Baptism. We become a new creation with infinite grace coming from God to be good. But it is up to us!

Once proclaimed by Pope Clement VII *Defender of the Faith*, King Henry's disobedience to the Chair of Peter resulted in other splinters predictably wrenching away from that *first* splinter. Jesus' Cross would be further fragmented; The Church of England would give birth to the *Quakers*, the *Methodists*, the *Episcopalians*, the *Pentecostals* and more, with discontentment breeding dissatisfaction, and dissatisfaction bringing about division, the disenchanted forming other churches, and then others forming branches of *those* churches, until the house divided against itself might have fallen, except God is Love and He keeps on loving us, no matter how much we try to abort His Will.

How can we know what Anglicans believe?

In England the Anglican Church, otherwise known as the Church of England, is still run by the state. In countries where British rule has existed, you will find this a major religion, but it can be found in most countries to some extent. The arms of the Anglican Church have been pulled apart, with Calvinism[38] on one side and the people's heartfelt desire to be part of the Catholic Church on the other. It has been fragmented to such a degree that if you asked 100 Anglicans what they believe, you would get 100 different answers.

[This is in no way a criticism, because with the flurry of dissenting theologians in our Church today spouting their own form of Catholicism it is difficult for the average Catholic or non-Catholic, to determine the true teachings of the Catholic Church.]

We can only *endeavor* to share what the Church of England was originally called to preach, as per Elizabeth I and her thirty-nine articles, which are still part of the official *Book of Common Prayer* of the Anglican Church.

When the Six Articles Act had been declared in 1539, it was formulated and executed with the supreme authority of the Crown, King Henry VIII. As Henry never stopped loving Mother Church, nor considered himself and England anything but Catholic, it defined six beliefs strongly *Catholic*. For Catholics or Protestants to challenge or contest any part of this Act was to be open to punishment - that of being burned alive at the stake.

But Henry died, and the Crown passed on to his son Edward VI. Whereupon Archbishop Cranmer, now free to undermine the Church under this poor sick puppet King, in 1553 did away with King Henry's Six Articles and issued his own *Forty-two* Articles. With this Act, so infused with Protestantism, *Lutheran and Calvinist* theology took over, undermining all the Catholic Dogmas that Henry's Six Articles had upheld. It waged war not only on Catholicism but on Protestants considered *extreme*, like Anabaptists. The Act was later reduced to thirty-nine articles. The damage was done and although Cranmer died a heretic, his infamy lasted almost 500 years. We say 500 years, because our hearts long and pray that our brothers and sisters return *Home* soon. We love and claim them back to Mother Church.

When Edward died, the Crown passed on to Henry's daughter[39] Mary Tudor and with this new Regent the return of the Catholic Faith. But with her death, the reign of

England and the Church of England passed on to Elizabeth. Back came Calvinist and Lutheran theology! Although Henry was responsible for repressing over 600 monasteries in order to fill his royal coffers and ordered the execution of bishops, priests, monks, nobles, and women, King Henry VIII, with the exception of disobedience to the Pope, defended and upheld all the Dogmas of the Church:

- Communion under one Specie,
- Confession
- Priesthood Celibacy
- Masses for the dead
- Belief in Transubstantiation

Not only did Henry fight efforts to make the Church of England Protestant, under him Cranmer had to tow the line, at least in public, to the degree he consented to send his *Lutheran wife*[40] and *children* back to Germany.

Under Henry, priests continued to celebrate true Roman Catholic Masses, and bishops continued to ordain *valid* priests.

After Henry, all this disappeared with the influx of foreigners moving into England with their Protestant ideology of:

- *Justification through faith alone,*
- *sola scriptura,*[41]
- *the elimination of 5 of the Sacraments,*
- *married priests,*
- *doing away with the Mass,*
- *iconoclasm,* thereby justifying the destruction of stained glass windows depicting the life of Jesus and Mary and that of the Saints, replacing them with Calvinistic themes having nothing to do with the *visible* Catholic Church of the past of the English. All the beautiful art disappeared from the churches.

Till today these Thirty-nine Articles, dating back to

Queen Elizabeth's time, are the official beliefs of the Church of England.[42] Some of their tenets are:

(1) Holy Scripture contains all that is necessary for salvation.

(2) Only that part of the Creed which has been proven by Holy Scripture is to be accepted.

(3) General Councils are not to be considered infallible.

(4) They deny *Transubstantiation* where Catholics believe that the host is no longer bread but the *Body, Blood, Soul and Divinity of Jesus Christ Himself*; and the wine no longer wine but the Body, Blood, Soul and Divinity of Jesus Christ.

(5) They discarded and denied all Catholic teachings on:

Purgatory,

Indulgences,

praying to Jesus through the intercession of Mother Mary and the Saints, declaring them all *"false and repugnant to the Lord."*[43]

(6) They referred to the Mass as *"a forged fable and dangerous deceit."*[44]

(7) First the Articles declared the King to be *Supreme Head of the Church of England and Ireland* and then in Elizabeth's time it was changed to: *"the Queen's Majesty"* has the *supreme power over all Ecclesiastical and Civil matters of the Realm.*

(8) It further adds that no foreign head has any authority over the Church and Realm, including the Pope.

(9) But it did include most of the following fundamental Christian teachings:

(a) *The Holy Trinity,*

(b) *The Incarnation,*

(c) *Our Redemption* received through Jesus Christ.

(d) Only two of the seven Sacraments accepted by the Roman Catholic Church: *Baptism*[45] and the *Lord's Supper.*[46]

Anglicans are no longer required to strictly adhere to these Articles, but only not to publicly attack them. Finding these Articles so inconsistent with the Church founded by Jesus, John Henry Newman made his decision to leave the Anglican Church and join the Roman Catholic Church. May his intercession unite us once and for all.

Over the years the Church of England lost many of its members to such churches as the Baptist, Congregationalist, Quaker, and Presbyterian. The Church of England began through the Oxford Movement to return to the Catholic Heritage of their ancestors with a new Sacramental life, a greater appreciation for the Church. This was the flicker of a small flame that lighted the way for the Church to return partially to its roots by forming the *High Church* or *Anglo-Catholic Church*. One who spearheaded the movement was John Henry Newman who later converted to the Catholic Church and died a Cardinal at age 89.

Most *Episcopalians*, an offshoot from the Church of England will tell you that they believe in all that is contained in the Nicene and Apostles Creed, but to what degree depends on which shoot of the Church of England Tree they are.

Contrary to their Protestant *Episcopalian* brothers and sisters, *Anglicans:*
- tend to lean more toward the teachings of the Catholic Church;
- they call their priests - Father,
- and although at their priests' ordination they profess that all that is necessary for salvation is the Bible, you will find that not all Anglican priests preach "*sola Scriptura.*"
- Although Anglicans do not say they believe in Purgatory, they do believe in what they call *a state of purification.*
- Some say that they believe in the Seven Sacraments,
- the Real Presence of Jesus in the Eucharist, depending on which Anglican you speak to. Some believe as we do that during the consecration, the bread turns into the Body, Blood, Soul and Divinity of Jesus Christ. But, as "Pope Leo XIII

declared in 1896, in his *Apostolicae Curae*, Anglican Orders are `absolutely null and utterly void'* because of the defect in the intention of the ordaining prelate or bishop, and especially because of the severe defect in the form for the Rite of Ordination."[47]

- fasting and abstinence,
- confession to a priest and receiving absolution from their sins in the Sacrament of Penance (Again as this faculty was only granted to the Apostles and those who succeeded them in unbroken succession, their absolution would not be binding.)[48]
- they say prayers and have Masses said for the dead as we Catholics do;
- they go on retreats;
- they pray for the intercession of Mother Mary and the Saints;
- they recite the Rosary;
- they make the Sign of the cross;
- they genuflect before entering a pew.

There are Confraternities and Guilds praying for the unification of the Anglican church with the Catholic Church.

Over the years Anglicans have revived religious orders for men and women. Some are dedicated to the recitation of the Rosary, to adoration of the Real Presence of Jesus in the Eucharist and etc.

Their cross is being under bishops they consider heretical. Their bishops are elected by the clergy and laity of the diocese, and many lean more to Protestantism. The Anglo-Catholics have repeatedly requested *Protestant* be removed as part of the official title of the Episcopalian Church, but to no avail.

There had been talk about reuniting the Church of England with the Roman Catholic Church, but the ordination of women within the Anglican Church put an end to that.

Pope Paul VI

But the positive that arose from the ashes of that imprudent negative is the thousands of Anglicans and Episcopalians who are flocking to the Catholic Church.

Disobedience breeds disobedience. Henry disobeyed his Pope, and then after his death his daughter Elizabeth disobeyed him. Now centuries later not even Elizabeth would recognize *her* Church. The Church Henry loved has become so splintered, so divided by so many differences, if he were to rise from the dead today, he would weep because he would no longer recognize the Church he had known. And so there are still those in England today who, like him, love all that is Catholic but are often dictated to and persecuted by those who discourage, to the point of forbidding, some of their pious practices like the use of incense, hearing confession and etc. The war between Calvinism and Catholicism is not yet over. But I think the enemy of division had gone too far with the ordination of women in the Episcopalian Church. Anglicans are returning to the Catholic Church. Praise God!

In 1970, Pope Paul VI canonized 40 English martyrs, martyred between 1533 and 1680. These martyrs were merely *representative* of the more than 600 martyrs being considered for canonization. Because of the lack of resources, Mother Church chose only these 40 out of 199 English martyrs of that period who had already been beatified in 1886, 1895, and 1929, to be investigated thoroughly.

[Being friendly with some promulgators of processes

for Beatification and Canonization, we can attest to the amount of paper work and great research required, the thorough inspecting of each and every word spoken or written attributed to the candidates, as well as the type of life they led - its virtue and faithfulness to profession.]

The necessary two miracles needed by canon law to be declared a Saint were to be used for the entire group, rather than individually. Among them were the better known Margaret Clitherow, Cuthbert Mayne, Edmund Campion and Robert Southwell.

Close to Pope Paul VI's heart and papacy was ecumenism and the unification of the splinters of the Cross with Mother Church. It appeared this was beginning to look plausible, when Pope Paul VI announced the Canonization of these Martyrs and the Anglican Church objected strongly. But the voices and love of the Martyrs of England for their Church could not be stilled. They would cry out from every Catholic heart in England that beats. The Catholics in England have never left the Church. They have just been waiting to come Home, once again; and when they do, there will be such a glorious light coming from our Church, it will lead all our brothers and sisters back.

Come Home; we grieve until you brighten the doors of our churches once more.

Footnotes

[1]An honor bestowed on him by Pope Leo X

[2]begun in the Fourteenth and Fifteenth centuries in Italy to give justification to the Renaissance. It advocated giving credit to intellectualism over God or religion. Its form generated a controversy which led the way to the Reformation. For further information, read chapter on Sacraments in Trilogy Book I - *Treasures of the Church*

[3]*Defense of the Seven Sacraments*

[4]including the granting of Indulgences

[5]Friends and family members of Anne Boleyn

[6]King Henry VIII

[7]beginning with Peter our first Pope commissioned by Jesus Himself

[8]Anne Boleyn had had many affairs by the time Henry was seduced by her, although historians cannot explain the reason for his obvious obsession, as she was far from attractive and was known to be a shrew.

[9]The child was Elizabeth who was born somewhere around September of the following year, and one day would be Queen.

[10]chaplain to Anne Boleyn and her family in the court

[11]*The Catholic Church through the Ages* - Fr. Martin P. Harney, S.J.

[12]more about St. John Fisher and St. Thomas More in Bob and Penny Lord's book: *Martyrs They died for Christ.*

[13]*Lives of the Popes*

[14]An interdict is a censure that deprives the faithful, either lay or cleric, of certain spiritual benefits but permits them to remain in the Church. It can be *personal* or *local*. As this covered an entire territory it is considered *local* and although this interdict does not forbid the administration of the Sacraments to the dying, it does forbid, with certain exceptions, the celebration of any divine services in the territory.(The Catholic Encyclopedia - Broderick)

[15]the killing of the priest-delegate and the mother of another priest

[16]When Henry decided to do away with Anne Boleyn, he accused her of indiscretions with several men, including her brother. Although some historians believe that they only confessed under threat of a death sentence, they too went to their death, along with Anne Boleyn.

[17]Read chapter on the Eucharist in *Trilogy Book I Treasures of the Church* by Bob & Penny Lord

[18]The Catholic Church through the Ages - Fr. Martin P. Harney, S.J.

[19]Whose code? Certainly not Vatican Council II, as some claim.

[20]Archbishop Fulton J. Sheen called a dry martyrdom one where the martyr does not die, but lives an ongoing martyrdom through the persecutions suffered day in and day out. More about Martyrs in Bob and Penny's book: *Martyrs they died for Christ*, and on Archbishop Fulton J. Sheen in *Saints and other Powerful Men in the Church.*

[21]yielding more power than the Prime Minister of Britain, today

[22]St. Catherine of Siena, referring to all our Popes beginning with Peter till today. For more on St. Catherine, read Bob and Penny's book: *Saints and other Powerful Women in the Church.*

[23]The British Isles

[24]Protestantism

[25] *"He* (Jesus) *said to His disciples: `Temptations to sin are sure to come; but woe to him by whom they come! It would be better for him if a millstone were hung around his neck and he were cast into the sea, than that he should cause one of these little ones to sin.'"*Lk 17:1-2

[26]overturned or rescinded

[27]also known as Mary Queen of Scots

[28]He was the harsh, determined, uncompromising instrument who was responsible for changing England from Catholic to Protestant.

[29]Using ethnic cleansing in Bosnia-Herzegovina (formerly Yugoslavia), one religious body waged a war against another with the focus of annihilating them once and for all.

[30]as a sponsor or instructor

[31]underlined by authors to emphasize reference

[32]Catechism of the Catholic Church #814, #815

[33]Catechism of the Catholic Church #2120

[34]Catechism of the Catholic Church #1413

[35]Mt 2:18

[36]Fifth Century

[37]her priests, her missionaries

[38]which infiltrated the church during Edward's and most especially Elizabeth's reign

[39]by Catherine of Aragon

[40]secret wife

[41]primacy accorded to Scripture over all other sources of doctrinal authority

[42]Although it is based on who you ask,

[43]New Catholic Encyclopedia - Book 14

[44]New Catholic Encyclopedia - Book 14

[45]Matthew Parker whom Elizabeth appointed Archbishop of Canterbury in 1559, defined the doctrines of the Church of England and the Advertisements (1556) which ordered the wearing of the surplice instead of vestments and *forbade the Sign of the Cross in Baptism.*

[46]under Parker's original 39 Articles, Article 29 read *"Of the Wicked which eat not the Body of Christ"* referring to the Eucharist. Not even Elizabeth would allow this to remain, fearful of what the Catholics in England would say. Instead she added Article 20 which read that the Crown had authority over all rites and ceremonies. She would later make it punishable by death for attending a Catholic Mass.

[47] Catholic History - Our Sunday Visitor

[48]refer to Pope Leo XII's *Apostolicae Curae*

Religious Wars

Battles Waged for and against the Church

As we said in the previous chapter, men of this age believed and fought for the Faith. Jesus would not have vomited out one of them, the wise or the unwise. They all felt strongly about their beliefs, and all were ready to do what it took to practice what they believed and lead others to believe with them. Feelings ran high, emotions feverish, the climate became volatile with horrible disregard for life and property on both sides. Once the gates of hell were open, the enemy of God was loose and he used God's children against each other; the plan - a house divided sure to crumble and fall. Only because Jesus made a promise that hell would not prevail against His Church does she still stand, her Lord alive on her altars and in her Tabernacles.

Sadly, in most instances, the fate of the Church in various countries in Northern Europe were decided by these Religious Wars. The victory of one political group determined whether Catholicism or Protestantism would rule in that area. That determination was the deciding factor of what religion the people would embrace from that time until modern times.

Four wars of Religion were fought! They were: The *Huguenot Wars* in France, the *Revolution* in the Netherlands, the *Battle* waged in Britain, and the *Thirty Years War* in Germany.

The Huguenot Wars

It was 1562, and we find the Church in France ready to do battle for her children. The eldest daughter of the Church, France was always a stronghold of Catholicism, giving to the Church many of her greatest Saints. And she was under attack! The Huguenot Wars were important battles, which each side needed to win. For as France went, most of northern Europe would go. France was a leader and widely respected in the secular world; therefore it stands to reason she could possibly lead other nations *spiritually* to remain Catholic or fall into Calvinism.

The Huguenot Wars consisted of *three* forces battling for France, with the north countries of Europe in their sights.

The *first* were Calvinists who wanted France to be solely and exclusively Protestant. Their ranks, as we will see throughout the battles to destroy the Church, were filled with a tiny three percent of the people of France. But they were the powerful few - princes and royalty who had much land and wanted to realize more by taking Papal Lands away from the Church. With position comes power, with power influence, and so they were a force to be reckoned with. All they needed to have complete victory in France was the help of the royalty in Germany, Holland and England.

The *second* force were the Catholics, born Catholics, Catholics like generations of Frenchmen before them, faithful to the death if necessary to the Church of their ancestors. They were the great *majority* of Frenchmen who wanted nothing less than a Catholic France for themselves and their children. Now the Dukes of Lorraine were nobility *faithful* to the Church, but they did not have the love and full allegiance of the people.[1] However, when Frenchmen at large became aware that the fight was whether the Church would live or die in France, they all quickly united behind the Dukes of Lorraine and became one, Mother Church always uniting her family.

The *third* force was filled with those motivated by lust for power and never-satisfying greed. It encompassed those few who ran the government and therefore wanted neither Catholicism nor Calvinism to be the dominating force in

France. This group was headed by the ambitious Queen Mother Catherine de Medici who would do anything to fulfill her lifelong ambition to keep one or another of her pathetic sons seated on the throne of France. This group went about pitting one against

Catherine de Medici

the other: the Huguenots against the Catholics, and then the Catholics against the Huguenots, aiding the losing side so that the battle would continue, weakening religion in its wake and its influence over the people.

The Huguenot Wars lasted thirty-one years. We have always contended that all wars are religious wars, the enemy of God causing discord, entreating brother to kill brother. This, like most wars, was a series of bloody battles filled with the massacre of the innocent along with the guilty, the blood of men, women and children, irrespective of age, flowing through the streets. As is true with most wars, these wars were no less maneuvered by heads of governments, in this case Catherine de Medici, to bring about her own ambitions at the reckless sacrifice of the young and the blameless.

There were casualties on both sides. The Massacre of St. Bartholomew's Eve (1572) was the most notorious and bloodiest of the Huguenot wars. It was waged at the hands of Catherine to put her son Charles IX on the throne, in accord with the House of Guise, a Catholic influential family.

Catholics were not involved; it was the Queen's men. But as it was the merciless slaughtering of Calvinists, the Church has wrongfully been accused by Protestants of this crime, to this day. No mention has ever been made that many years preceding the devastating travesty of St. Bartholomew's Eve, thousands upon thousands of priests and religious had been annihilated.

Whenever the Calvinists attacked, they left not a sign of the Catholic Faith behind them. Not satisfied to kill priests and religious, they sacked churches and monasteries, and destroyed the priceless ancient paintings depicting the life of Jesus, Mary and the Saints in an all-out campaign to wipe the Church off the face of the earth. But the final blow was when they desecrated the Eucharist in many unspeakable ways. The Calvinists wounded the faithful more, when they forced them to stand by and watch Our Lord present in the Eucharist being crushed under the heels of their boots, than when they pierced them and their loved ones with their blood-stained swords.

What the Calvinists could not accomplish, could have been brought to fruition with the ascendancy of Henry IV, a Huguenot prince, to the throne. But the Church triumphed! King Henry asked for absolution, having been formerly Catholic, and made his Profession of Faith in 1593. In 1598, he issued the Edict of Nantes, reinstating property, churches and monasteries to the Church. The Huguenot Wars ended. The Huguenots were allowed to practice Calvinism. But although they remained a menacing force, the Catholic Church was once again Mother of France, her beloved eldest daughter. Louis XIII, a devout Catholic, ascended to the throne in 1610 and the Church was assured of its place in France. But most credit must be given to the loyalty of the French majority who willingly fought and died for the Church they loved. The suffering they endured only made them stronger. Had they taken their Church for granted and almost lost her? Do we have to almost lose our Church to appreciate and revere her, defend her, live and die for her?

The battle of the Netherlands

The world has always been small; war is like a tiny snowball rolling down a mountain gaining, growing into a mass causing an avalanche. As the Huguenot Wars were raging in France, the Church was being attacked on another front - in the Netherlands, an area filled with holy and reverent Catholics who spoke Dutch, Flemish and French.[2] To really understand how these deeply faithful Catholics could lose the Faith, we have to look at the history of the times. Here again, we find the world and the Church intertwined unwittingly in a critical battle.

The Netherlands was torn and divided politically. On the one hand, there was the question, should they remain under the Hapsburg Kings of Spain or become an independent nation with their own regent; and on the other hand, should they remain Catholic or become Calvinist? The tentacles of Lutheranism from Germany and Calvinism from France had already been making dangerous inroads in their midst.

Although conditions in the Church in the Netherlands were not like those that existed in Germany, France and England, there were *some* abuses. But more than the *few* priests and religious who had forgotten their vows, there were the strong, faithful and holy *majority* of priests and religious who did not deserve the mass anti-clericalism being waged against them and the Church. For some reason, man can always get away with persecuting the Church to accomplish his own goals and the unknowing faithful are always the victims. Pamphlets were widely circulated blasting all we Catholics hold dear.

Brutal and radical *Humanism* was the reigning queen of the ball. Nothing and no one was spared!

Using the media of its time,[3] the in-sport of the day was the flagrant contempt of the *Sacraments*.

There was a prevailing movement to discredit the Church, using deceptive theology attacking the granting of *Indulgences*.

Iconoclasm cropped its ugly head again, the faithful at large unaware it was an old heresy condemned centuries before, as *Sacramentals* came under attack.

Bob and Penny Lord on Pilgrimage to the Shrines of Europe

The tradition of going on *Pilgrimage*, an ancient custom dating back to the Old Testament, was assailed as superstition - alleging this was to gain special favors *solely* through the visiting of the Shrines.[4]

Mother Mary, the Saints and the Angels were placed on the unemployment line. By invoking their intercession, the Church was accused of placing them on a level with Jesus (or worse granting them Divinity).

Those who knew better joined the enemies of the Church by participating in the frivolity of the day, attending plays which made sport of mocking the Pope and the Church. And no one did anything about it. Sound familiar? The majority were not privy to this sport, and so they were not initially affected. But their leaders were and they would bring about this tragic travesty either by word or the sword!

The Church in the Netherlands was being attacked from all sides: From Germany with the Lutherans, from England with Protestantism, and France with Calvinism. As some of those otherwise faithful to the Catholic Church, considered Catholicism a link to Catholic *Spain*, and they were striving for *independence* from Spain, we can see an impending crisis! So once again, God and His Church had to take a back seat to *the false god of Nationalism.*

But the battle was not yet lost! Between Charles the V with his edicts against heresy, and the sound instruction from those of the University of Louvain, the Netherlands remained Catholic *for a while.* Emperor Charles gave his son, King Philip of Spain, the low countries, including the Netherlands. This was not a popular move, as Philip had introduced *the Inquisition into Spain,* which frightened the people and kept a firm grip for Catholicism on the Netherlands.

William of Orange

Enter William, Prince of Orange, the instrument that would be used by *the enemy* to bring about division, splitting the area into Catholics and Protestants. Little did he know that ultimately this division would cause not only the *spiritual* but the *political and geographical*[5] dissection of the Netherlands. Now this had not been his objective; all that William wanted was to realize his ambition to rule *all* of the Netherlands. But once on a course, the course often runs away from the traveller and he is in for more than he bargained for. Had he known what his self-interest would

Philip II of Spain

eventually bring about, would he have forged ahead? William aspired and then his aspiring turned into conspiring against any and all that stood in his way.

Like his fellow princes, William of Orange knew how to play the game. He was always what we would call today *politically correct*. Because of his skillful politicking, he was given several provinces to rule. Although his plans were more widespread, he accepted, expediently pledging his undying loyalty to Philip II. But after Philip left for Spain, he used King Philip's[6] link to Spain and the Catholic Church to ascend the throne as King of the Netherlands; and as part of his plan, he championed *Protestantism*. But had he not been Catholic when he was part of Philip's court? Not particularly faithful to any philosophy, but a chameleon who could change his color at the drop of a hat, when William dealt with German princes in an attempt to get their cooperation, he conveniently became Lutheran. Was it expedient to be Calvinistic, well then go for it, and William did! He used fear with the people of the Netherlands, instilling suspicion and wariness that Philip would bring the dreaded Inquisition to the Netherlands.

Chaos and cruelty erupted causing a Religious Revolution which pitted brother against brother. Surrounding nations seeing the breakdown of the governing body and the disunity which resulted, took this opportunity to take over the divided kingdom. Knowing that he who speaks from the pulpit of God's House influences the people, Protestants from the British Isles, Lutherans from the German provinces, French Calvinists as well as those from Geneva all crossed the border and, in the name of wanting to give assistance and charity, converged on the unsuspecting. *To the strongest goes the spoils*; At the end, Calvinism won out.

But the Faith lived on! How do you wipe out that which has been imprinted on man's heart? Destroy! There was a wild senseless burning, desecrating of everything Catholic! Over 1,000 churches laid in ruin, victims of this rampage. As if the willful destruction of all the statues, paintings, vestments, sacramentaries, prayer books, and ancient priceless hand-printed, hand-painted Bibles were not enough, a heart rending desecration of the Blessed Sacrament was perpetrated throughout the kingdom.

The early Church Fathers said that without the Eucharist the Church would not have lasted the first 100 years. Over the years, the Lord, through Miracles of the Eucharist[7] has proven that the Eucharist is the Heart of the Church; without the Eucharist we have no life in us, we are dead. When they could not stop the faithful from believing with their lies, and then by the horrible desecration of Our Lord Jesus Present in His Body, Blood, Soul and Divinity in the Eucharist, then they systematically went about taking away the very instruments from whose hands the Eucharist comes to us during the Holy Mass; they killed the priests!

Still more than half Catholic, finally it was up to the people of the Netherlands to decide. They soon discovered, almost too late, that the battle had not been between the Spanish Philip II and William of Orange, as they had been led to believe, but between Catholicism and Calvinism! In 1578, after nineteen years of relentless attacks on the Church, seven of the provinces to the north formed one unified country called *the Dutch Republic* and, as they were now exclusively under the House of Orange, became strict Calvinists. As a result, tendering little sympathy or tolerance toward the small minority who remained Catholic, the persecution continued. The southern part of the Netherlands split from the north and remained Catholic, as it is largely so, till today.

What kind of a man was this William of Orange? There was a time I would have said, with the type of vacillation this man showed - switching sides at the drop of a hat, he could never have gotten elected to public office, but sadly history would have proven me wrong. There was a famous statesman who once said: *"You can fool some of the people all of the time, and you can fool all of the people some of the time, but you cannot fool all of the people all of the time."*[8] This great statesman must be turning in his grave! William was able to rend such destruction upon this once truly faithful Catholic people they would not only lose the Catholic Church they would eventually lose God.[9]

Let us in no way, lead you to believe this came to pass without the shedding of much blood. It took thirty years for the death of the Faith! Our brothers and sisters of the Netherlands will return to the Church they so loved and revered, because the blood of their ancestors cries out for their return to the Church. In parts of the Netherlands it has already begun.

The Catholic Battle in the British Isles

The British Isles consists of three nations, as it did at the time of the Religious Revolution: England, Ireland[10] and Scotland. The war was to rage on these islands for not thirty years, as it had in the rest of Europe, but for forty years - the length of Queen Elizabeth's reign of terror. The determining battle had to be waged in England, as England was a powerful nation. Because of her superior navy she was a dominate power in the North Sea and the English Channel, and as such she maintained a critical political position on the continent of Europe. It was crucial that *Protestantism* be victorious in England for the rest of Europe to be swallowed up.

The muscle of the Protestant war on Catholicism would be tested first on two nations of the British Isles considered less formidable. The decision was made: The battle had to be won at all costs in Scotland and Ireland!

Begin with Scotland!

Now in Scotland, those in favor of Protestantism were the minority; but being the nobility, they were a *powerful* minority. And as the nobles wielded more power than the monarchy who favored the Catholic Church, it was to be a tough time for all concerned. Again we have a story of greed and self-interest! By the take-over of monasteries and churches, the nobility stood to gain lands and treasures formerly donated to the Church by grateful kings and queens over the centuries. Now, as in other countries, the major population was strongly and faithfully Catholic. How would the nobles accomplish this without suffering grave consequences at the hands of the faithful? Recruit forceful, dynamic on-fire preachers who would be able to manipulate the mass populace into believing the Church was corrupt and that God had chosen *them* to bring the *true church* to them. Those recruited became recruiters and soon the movement began to succumb to such inflammatory preachers as John Knox.

Now it benefited Queen Elizabeth to cripple the Catholic Church in Scotland, as her aim for years had been to undermine Mary Queen of Scots' reign in Scotland. It was of deep concern to Elizabeth that many of her subjects believed that Mary and not Elizabeth was the rightful heir to the throne of England. This sword always hovering over Elizabeth, threatening her claim to the crown, she freely offered financial and military aid to those putting down the Catholic Church. By so doing, she judged she would critically diminish Mary Stuart's[11] influence in Scotland and squash any future claim she might have to the monarchy in England. Now, that Mary Stuart exercised no hint of claim to the throne was of no consequence; she was a threat in Elizabeth's mind and she had to be dealt with.

Queen Mary had been in France with her husband, heir to the French throne. When her husband died, she returned to Scotland. But she found herself much alone, as her staunch defender, her mother Mary of Guise had died. Try as she may, with the nobility the real power in Scotland, it was near impossible for Queen Mary to procure any form of religious freedom for her Catholic subjects in Scotland. The most she could get the nobles to grant her was token permission to have Mass said for her and her court *privately*. This was tenuous at best. All in all, it did not look good for the prospects of a Catholic Scotland.

Four years before Mary's return to Scotland, a covenant had been signed among the nobles to denounce and then completely destroy the Catholic Church. Under this covenant, they banished Catholic priests; and those who dared to remain in Scotland became fugitives facing imprisonment, torture and death. They replaced Catholic priests and the Mass with services filled with inflammatory anti-Catholic preaching by Protestant ministers, the likes of John Knox. As part of the complete obliteration of the presence of Catholicism, they followed their French Huguenot counterparts and Dutch Reform confreres across the Channel, and in the name of *Iconoclasm*[12] made a clean sweep, destroying sacred statues and paintings, ransacking churches and looting monasteries.

John Knox

The Lords of the Covenant, as they called themselves, called for a new Profession of Faith - a Declaration of *Calvinistic* Faith. It began with the nullification of all authority of the Pope over matters of Faith and Morals in Scotland. Then it revoked any and all concessions formerly allowed to Catholics in Scotland. Under this covenant, celebration of the Holy Mass became a crime, punishable by death after the third offense; and those churches or homes where the outlawed Mass was said, were confiscated.

The young queen tried desperately to keep the Faith alive. It got so bad that practicing her Faith within the confines of her royal quarters was little by little being denied her; her only solace was when she could steal away privately and pray. Her royal chambers no longer a haven, she was visited often by John Knox and required to listen attentively to tirades against her Church and false accusations against her personally. *This went on for seven years.* When her enemies began to accuse her of having been unfaithful to her husband and having had him killed, when she saw her friends one by one executed, alone and forlorn, she turned to her cousin Queen Elizabeth for asylum. A very sad, broken Queen Mary left for England.

Mary, Queen of Scots gone, the Religious War in Scotland was ended. The battle had been bravely fought, the blood of the brave still red on the moors, the official church of Scotland was no longer Catholic but Calvinistic or Presbyterian as it is called till today.

This was not the mandate of the people but of the powerful few who have always determined the fate of the many. But the Scots were loyal to the Faith of their ancestors and thirty years after the Parliament of 1560 which took away all rights of the Catholic Church, more than half the parish churches were still in the hands of Catholics. When they could not use their parish churches, they attended Mass and received the Sacraments in burned out monasteries and churches, continuing to practice their Faith in the face of imprisonment and ultimate death. But the day was to come when no more were churches in the hands of Catholics, Calvinist preachers taking possession of their pulpits and then their souls. Catholic priests no more, no one left to celebrate the Holy Mass, confer the Sacraments or instruct the children in the Faith, no more would church bells peel calling Catholics to Mass in Scotland.

The war goes to England

Mary Stuart was now in England, Elizabeth having granted her sanctuary. But the peace she felt would be short-lived! As many thought of Queen Mary as the hope of Catholicism returning to England; and since most looked upon her as the rightful heir of the throne, gossip of an overthrow of Queen Elizabeth was filtering through to the Queen, and Mary's fate and that of Catholicism was not looking too optimistic.

Catholics had endured ten years of Elizabeth's reign of terror, one filled with varied and horribly inhumane acts of persecution, short of wet martyrdom (which was later to follow). During this period, she exiled Catholic bishops replacing them with heretics, starved out priests faithful to the Church - all forms of income forbidden them, celebration of the Holy Mass was strictly prohibited with the threat of death and or imprisonment. Fines and heavy taxes were imposed on those who did not attend the new Protestant services; and that failing to bend the English will, they were jailed as having committed treason against the throne, Elizabeth having declared this the official church of the realm.

A revolt took place in the north of England, an heroic attempt to reinstate the Catholic Church and have Mary Stuart rightfully[13] ascend the throne. The colors[14] borne by the army were the Five Wounds of Jesus. The Church was reinstated to her rightful place in the north. The army marched on to the south to free the Catholics from their heretical captivity; but sadly the people of the South were not equipped to help them, and the promised help from Spain and the Catholic Netherlands never arrived. Elizabeth's well prepared Puritan Army in the South swiftly and mercilessly put down the revolt. Elizabeth's fury could not be contained as she went about inflicting unfathomable vengeance on the territories in the North, declaring martial law, executing 900 peasants and officers of the Army of the Five Wounds in one fell swoop. The aristocracy was not spared, as her one-sided courts tried and condemned them for treason. The Earl of Northumberland died a martyr's death for the Faith, representing the tens of thousands unknown and unsung who died rather than deny their Faith and Pope.[15]

Raids were perpetrated on homes at all hours of the

day and night by priest-hunters, looting and destroying that which they could not carry off. But this did not stop the yearning for the true Faith in the hearts of the faithful. Priests clandestinely travelled the countryside, administering the Sacraments and instructing the children until caught, tortured, imprisoned and executed. The throne made examples of them, often leaving their remains visible as a warning. This, instead of deterring the faithful, only strengthened them. The song *Faith of our Fathers* drew its inspiration from these Catholics who died rather than deny the Faith of their fathers.

The Religious Wars come to Ireland in 1562

Ireland - Land of Faith - Land of Martyrs

Being married to a man of Irish decent, I can attest to the fact this would not be an easy victory for the enemies of the Church. The Irish have the gift of *Holy Stubbornness*; try to move an Irishman when he does not want to be moved! *My heart is restless until it rests in Thee, Lord.* These laments of St. Augustine have been echoed by the faithful for centuries, but no more than by the Irishmen for the return of their Faith to the Emerald Isle.

St. Oliver Plunket
The last of the Irish Martyrs

All attempts to place Mary Stuart upon the throne having failed, Scotland was lost to the Faith. But during the battle over Scotland another war was being waged - over the souls of the faithful of Ireland! It hit Ireland three years after Elizabeth ascended the throne. It would mean for Ireland 41 years of Elizabeth and her wrath against the Catholic Church, the very one her father had defended against Luther.[16]

As part of her inheritance from her father King Henry VIII, she had been given the title of Queen of Ireland. As their Queen, whether they liked it or not, she had the power; and she was determined to use that power to divest the Irish of their Catholic Faith and force them to join the Church of England. I guess she did not know with whom she was dealing. The Gaelic-Irish who were the majority and the Anglo-Irish who were the minority were united in their love for Mother Church.

Now for the Gaelic-Irish, the Faith and who they were as a people were so completely intertwined you could not destroy the one without the other. Their language, their laws, their customs, their Gaelic culture which dated back to before Christ were all *one* with the Catholic Faith they embraced - one and inseparable. Elizabeth had only one recourse. Dialog was impossible - only military strength and extreme measures would bring about the complete capitulation of Ireland. Ireland fought! The blood of the Martyrs[17] flowed from 1562 until 1603.

The Irish waged three different battles against the overwhelming power of Elizabeth's forces. All three uprisings failed! But it was not because the Irish were outnumbered that they failed to defeat the enemy, it was the systematic annihilation of the people of Ireland - men, old and young, women of all ages, innocent babies and children either butchered mercilessly or starved to death. Along with the English soldiers' normal means of attack: guns and swords, standard weapons of warfare included scythes and sickles. These would be used to destroy crops and livestock they could not cart away from those Irish who would not bend to the will of the Queen rather than, as they believed, to the Will of God.

A well respected Englishman reported that in 1582, there were 30,000 Irishmen starved in a period of six months. On one of our pilgrimages we and our pilgrims stood in just *one* of the fields where thousands of Irishmen had been buried: The sign read *Famine Grave*. As we prayed with our priests, in that horrible silence we could still hear the cries of the parents who had buried their children, their bellies still swollen from starvation. As I write, I remember and the tears begin to flow once more. As Bob has so often said at Auschwitz, at a former abortion clinic, and at this field: *"You had to be there."*

We walked deep into another field. Horses were peacefully grazing. We quietly approached an Altar Stone. It was one of the temporary altars that the Irish would set

Mass Rock - Used to say Mass during the Penal times in Ireland

up, a lookout on the hillside poised to warn the priest and the faithful of an approaching English army. The Irish would stack stones and form an altar that could be quickly disassembled, so the enemy would not be aware a Mass had been celebrated there.[18] Should they get caught, the priest would be tortured and finally executed, the faithful would lose their homes and any form of inheritance they were supposed to receive would go to Protestant relatives. All I could think was: How would we handle this type of persecution? Oh dear Lord, put us not to the test, we beg You.

Finally hardly an Irishman alive, Ireland succumbed! For Elizabeth this had to be an empty victory. Her generals reported that her subjects in Ireland were now solely comprised of ashes and dead carcasses. But they were wrong! The Irish did not fail and the Church did not die! She rose, once again from the ashes. The carcasses the generals spoke of were those of martyrs whose blood nourished the Church in Ireland. The Martyrs did not die in vain. More rose up to live for the Faith and if need be die for her.

Young Irishmen were spirited out of Ireland to Catholic

countries where they studied for the Priesthood and then returned to bring the Sacraments and the Faith to the Irish, often suffering martyrdom when caught. They knew the price and yet they came, and more came, and the Faith in Ireland was stronger than ever.

But it would appear that what the *Penal Times*[19] (as this period was called), could not do, sadly the media of today is doing. To the foolish, it looks as if the Irish are losing their Faith. But I know, as well as I know my Bob, they will rise again Catholic to the core.

Thirty Years War - Holy Roman Empire

Europe is no longer Holy,
> no longer Roman,
> > no longer an Empire.

Of all the battles waged, of all the wars fought, this the fourth war, was the most ferocious and deadly. Twenty years passed; the other three wars had ended, and the battle was waging once again, only this would be the one that would deal the final blow to Catholicism and finally Christianity in much of Northern Europe.

The Holy Roman Empire of the Germans, as it was originally named, was made up of over 300 little kingdoms. All these principalities and duchies, including even dioceses, were dominated by German princes; only a few scattered cities were self-governed. The German part of the title was not really given because it was composed of a majority of Germans, but because it was ruled by German princes. In addition, these princes not only elected the new Emperor of the Holy Empire, they were the ones who presented him to the Pope to be crowned by His Holiness.

It was called the *Holy* Roman Empire because at its inception its primary focus had been the defense of the Roman Catholic Church and her Holy Vicar-the Pope. But sadly once formed, there is a tendency to forget the primary purpose, and there is such change from the first concept of how things might be, you wonder what they were thinking in the first place. To try to give them credit, possibly the Empire ran away with itself and its leaders. History has proven over and over again that this often happens with all forms of revolution.

Although it was founded originally by Otto I, a German King in 962,[20] it was called *The Roman* Empire because it was to be a continuance of the once powerful earlier *Roman Empire*. But unlike the original it could hardly have been called an Empire, as it had very little influence anywhere but in a limited area in Austria. For the century prior to the Seventeenth when all hell broke loose, the crown of the Emperor was worn by a member of the Catholic Hapsburgs, the Archduke of Austria. As the tempest of the storm had been stirred up by Luther, followed by Calvin and Jansen, soon the *Protestant* princes were challenging the *Catholic* Archduke for the crown of the Empire. It has been widely believed that it was this irreconcilable controversy which started the Thirty Year War.

By 1618, the Empire was no longer Holy and no longer a defender of the Church or the Pope. On the contrary, more than half the Empire had become staunchly *anti-papal*. This war, the most violent of all four wars, lasted until 1648, fifty years after the wars of the French Huguenots, Dutch Calvinists, and English Anglicans had ended. There were many reasons why this war erupted so many years after those in other areas. Compromises had been made to avert war. The Religious *Peace of Augsburg* in 1555 left the lands, they had taken from the Church, in the hands of the Lutheran princes. It further conceded that the prince and the prince alone decided the religion of his peasants. This treaty like all treaties that settle matters by appeasement just left for another day that which should have been resolved immediately. Tyranny is like a miser with gold - no power is enough. Not satisfied with retaining what they had stolen, the Lutheran princes wanted more Church property. The Church lost more dioceses and more monasteries. The Emperors who followed Charles V were too weak to protect Catholic rights and so, the Empire became more and more separated from Mother Church.

Another reason that wholesale war was not waged was that Protestant princes began to argue among themselves. When the treaty[21] had been drawn up, it was strictly between Lutherans and Catholics, the Calvinists a small minority at the time. But twenty years later, this most zealous group had grown to substantial numbers and insisted they be included. Now the Lutherans and the Calvinists had had some very heated arguments concerning differences in dogmas, over the years. Lutherans and Catholics had lived for years in comparative peace and harmony. Now here were the Calvinist princes insisting *they* be in charge of *reforming* the Catholics, with the ultimate goal - the fall of Catholicism. This was not the only reason Lutherans reacted strongly to the Calvinist princes' demands: The Calvinists were standing on the articles of the treaty which stated that since the prince of a state determines the religion and they had taken over some Lutheran areas, they should now be no longer Lutheran, but Calvinist states! The Lutherans insisted the Calvinists were not included in the treaty, so it did not apply to them and their rights. This only served to add fuel to the fire!

While all this was going on, God was rounding up powerful men and women to defend His Church - *New life* was being breathed into Catholicism in Germany! The Church was rising from the ashes. Decrees from the Council of Trent were published; new breviaries were being used; reform was happening in many Religious Orders which had grown lax; many young men were stepping forward dedicating their lives to the priesthood; new orthodox seminaries were bringing forth holy priests who became holy prelates who lead the faithful to holiness; there was a revival going on in Germany and it was exciting! Three Bavarian dukes joined in and the tide of Protestantism was stemmed. Whole areas returned to the Catholic Church. Faithful Laity and Religious worked together and much of Germany was reclaimed for the Church. And this, in spite of an Archbishop (who had defected to Calvinism) and the efforts of his wife (who just happened to be an ex-nun) to turn the Archdiocese of Cologne into a lay Calvinist principality.

Not getting their way, the Calvinists decided to take matters into their own hands and take up arms. In an attempt to draw Lutherans, they called themselves the *Evangelical Union*. But most Lutheran princes did not join them. England joined the fray on the side of the Calvinists, adding support from her entire United Kingdom. Then a year later to help Catholics defend themselves against the Calvinists, Maxmilian, the Catholic Duke of Bavaria formed a *Catholic League*. He was joined by the three Bishops of Mainz, Trier and Cologne[22] prince-bishops, and abbots with the Pope and the King of Spain lending *financial* support.

There were five stages of this war. The first three battles were waged by the Calvinists and their allies against Catholics. The Catholics were joined by the Imperialists who entered the war in the third stage and together they successfully defeated the Calvinists and their allies. Had the war ended at that time, more than two thirds of Germany would have remained Catholic. But Emperor Ferdinand issued the *Edict of Restitution* whereby all Protestant princes were required to return all properties, gained through a violation of the Peace Treaty of Augsburg, to the original title holders: dioceses and monasteries. Now, although he

was acting within the law of
the Treaty, this action was to
keep a brutal war brewing for
another 19 years.

Sweden joined in the
melee, adding military
strength and resources to the
Calvinists. Cardinal
Richilieu, more a statesman
of France than a Catholic
Cardinal, was responsible for
France sending additional
reinforcements to the
Calvinists. He justified this
action against the Church he
had pledged to defend, with

Cardinal Richilieu

the worldly, nationalistic-based justification: He was coming
against the Hapsburgs! Thanks to him and all the other aid
the Calvinists received, the Catholics and the Imperialists
were defeated. *"To the victor belongs the spoils"* was a
motto the Calvinist forces along with their allies, personified
as they went on a wild rampage, pilfering, looting, burning
everything they could not carry away. And when things
material were all despoiled, they went after women and
children, committing the most brutal atrocities. Three fourths
of the uninvolved, innocent German peasantry died either
as victims of this horrible war or casualties of a pestilence
resulting from diseases brought into the area by mercenaries
and those from other parts.

Both sides weary and wasting away, a new treaty was
formed: *The Peace of Westphalia*. The ongoing controversies
over the Peace of Augsburg were ironed out in the new treaty.
With it, no longer were bishops in Germany at risk of losing
Church property. The Catholic Church was stronger than

ever, persecution having given the people a new awareness of the Treasure they had in their midst. No longer would they take their Church for granted! The agreement that came about as a result of the treaty split Germany into two equal parts, the North remaining *Protestant* and the South and West completely *Catholic*.[23] It has remained so for the last three hundred years.

This part of our book is very dear to me, as my Aunt Eva (and godmother) was from Southern Germany, and a stronger more devout and pious Catholic one would be hard pressed to find.

Wars over, the Church faces the enemy within

The enemy of God never sleeps! The peace that The Treaty of Westphalia was supposed to bring about was short-lived. The world came crashing in! *Secularism*, the false god of the world took priority over *Spirituality* and the One True God. The peace and fellowship between Christians was a candle whose wick was so short, its light quickly went out. Protestants did not allow Catholics to live in their states, and those principalities that were Catholic had governments that interfered with the Church to the degree they had veto power over the Cardinals' choice of a Pope!

Dear God, you would think that after all the wars and bloodshed, the blood of martyrs still visible, at least Catholics could live in harmony with each other. But it is always those few with self-interest, the serpent still luring God's creation with promises of grandeur, who will do anything to realize the enemy's promise of being their own god on earth. *Nationalism* reared its ugly head! Schisms were threatened by individual states if their wishes were not adhered to by the Pope. The attacks on the Papacy, infiltrating the Church itself, gave birth to heresies like Gallicanism and Jansenism. But to counteract those who were against the Barque of

Peter[24] God raised up men and women who heard the call to holiness and said yes. It was Abraham all over again bargaining with God: *And what if there are only 10 good men?*[25]

France, as well as being beloved daughter of the Church, became one of the most respected, most powerful nations in the world, God blessing France for her undying loyalty. But in addition to her many laudatory titles, it would be fitting to call her *Mother of the Counter-Reformation*, for having given to the Church such faithful children in the Seventeenth Century to counteract those who had gone astray: *St. Francis de Sales, St. John Eudes, St. Vincent de Paul, and St. Margaret Mary Alacoque*, to mention a few.

There can be peace on earth, the Peace that Jesus promised! Our Church's Religious with their faithfulness to Mother Church and their vocations - men ordained to lives as bishops and priests, men who took their vows as brothers, and women who donned holy veils as Brides of Christ, will hold up a mirror of holiness for the whole world to look into and the world will see how Jesus is calling us *all* to holiness in our stations in life. *Men* of the laity will look into this mirror, and they will see a reflection of faithfulness that will lead them to be faithful to their vocations as Catholics, as brothers, sons, husbands, and fathers. Just as we women desire to be more like our role model Mother Mary, when we look into this mirror we will see chaste and holy nuns, models for us to imitate and we will follow, as we endeavor to live our lives of fidelity and devotion to our families, our fathers and mothers, our spouses, our children, our parish communities.

At our first Marriage Encounter weekend, we heard that we were to *revere* our spouses. I never thought of revering anyone but Our Lord and His Mother; but that weekend, I looked at my spouse with different eyes, and I have never

Saints of the Counter-Reformation

St. Vincent de Paul

St. Francis de Sales

St. Teresa of Avila

St. Margaret Mary Alacoque

stopped looking at him except with the *new* eyes that the Holy spirit gave me that weekend. We either lead each other to Heaven or hell. What an awesome, terrifying opportunity and responsibility our Lord shares with us. Will we fail? Yes, but we will try again, falling twelve times and getting up thirteen.[26]

A very interesting movement that had a great impact on the reform and consequent holiness of the Church was one founded and directed by the Laity. It was the *Company of the Blessed Sacrament.* No matter what we write about, it always comes back to the Eucharist. One day at Holy Mass, when the Bishops of the United States were discussing taking away some of our Holy Days dedicated to the Blessed Mother, I still remember how distraught we all were when we turned to our priest.[27] [Wherever he is, I hope he reads this.] It was his words that lifted us up and gave us new hope. Suddenly we no longer felt helpless and hopeless. He said: *"It has always been the laity that has fostered and kept devotions alive in the Church, not the hierarchy."* So when some priest or bishop tells you that adoring the Blessed Sacrament is not in keeping with Vatican Council II or whatever new tall tale they are manufacturing, remember no one can stop you from adoring your Lord so present in the Blessed Sacrament, except yourself falling for the lie.

I pray that as you read this Trilogy and our book on the *Martyrs who died for Christ* and His Church, you will remember the price paid for our Church by those who have gone before and you won't let anyone take Our Church and her Treasures away from you, especially the Gift of Our Lord present in the Eucharist and his Mother Mary.

France began sending young men - priests and *donnés*[28] to the New World to bring Jesus and His Church to the Native-Americans. When these men said goodby to their mothers and fathers, they all knew they would come back

Martyrs for the Faith and they all said Yes! The Roll Call unfurls with such Jesuit missionaries of the Seventeenth Century as:

St. Isaac Jogues,

St. John de Brébuf, St. Antony Daniel,

St. Gabriel Lalemant, St. Charles Garnier,

St. Noel Chabanal,

St. René Goupil,

St. John Lalande,

giving their lives for the Church. As we researched our book on the Martyrs, we had a recurring thought that must challenge non-believers: *Did they die for a piece of bread?*

Jansenism - Calvinistic Catholicism
Seventeenth Century

"Tower of Jansenius" In this tower at the University of Louvain, Jansen wrote part of his work on grace.

Bishop Cornelius Otto Jansen, better known by his Latin name of *Jansenius* was a pious and austere bishop, deeply attached to the Church. He defended the Church against Richilieu and his alliances with the Protestants. Bishop Jansen published many papers, fighting the Protestantism infiltrating Europe. He made one mistake and that mistake caused a division in the Church that began after his death, but lived on into the next century.

There are no wounds so painful, so piercing the Heart of Jesus as when one of His apostles falls into error.

Again, heresy is here and spreading wildly in Europe and what is at the bottom of it, a book written by a bishop -

Cornelius Jansen, Bishop of Ypres, once a professor of the much respected University of Louvain.[29] It all started with his book *Augustinus* which was filled with heretical dogmas based on his mis-interpretations of St. Augustine's writings. Never desiring to be disobedient, on his deathbed, he said that he eagerly awaited and would abide by the findings of Mother Church. But he was not to rest in peace. Two years after his death, Abbé St. Cyran, an associate of Jansen published his book in Paris and began preaching Jansen's heretical dogmas on morality and spirituality.

A few elitists were too proud to accept the ancient teachings of the Church; this included priests, nuns, and laity coming from the most influential circle naturally. [*To whom much is given, much will be required.* Why is it that those who are so gifted by the Lord and have an opportunity to lead souls to Paradise, most often choose the path to eternal damnation?]

This dangerous sect that attracted the most influential people plagued the Church for over 100 years. One of the features of this sect was their severely austere lifestyle in contrast to the very *laissez-faire* lifestyle so prevalent in French society. [Is this not what is happening to our young, today? Are they not swapping dances, beach parties and ski trips that many in our Church are offering for a more rigorous life in a cult? The young have always wanted to be challenged.]

It seems the more we delve into the things that separate us from our brothers and sisters in Christ, we come up with: *Grace* and *Free Will*! We in the Catholic Church are taught and believe that:

God's Grace is absolutely necessary for salvation;
God wishes all men to be saved;
God gives to each man sufficient Grace to be saved;
God, since He endows man with Free Will, makes the

Pope Pius X

efficacy (power) *of His saving Will depend on man's cooperation with it.*[30]

Jansenism taught that God chose a *few* to be saved, that God does not will all men to be saved-only a small minority, that He did not die for all-only that small minority He predestined to be saved. It all is one thread that leads us to Heaven with God's Truth or hell with man's lies. With these Jansenist heresies, there is no hope in prayer to Jesus, directly or through Mary and the Saints. Jansen's dogma points back to Calvin's no hope, no help dogma of predestination.[31]

What was Jansenism going to attack next? Why the Sacraments, of course, especially the Eucharist and the Sacrament of Penance. First, the Jansenists preached that receiving Holy Communion frequently should be forbidden. [Isn't it funny that in the early 1900s, when Modernism was spreading wildly among the priesthood, St. Pope Pius X[32] encouraged *frequent Communion*. The Pope knew that the only way we the Church could survive the deadly virus of Modernism,[33] one of the most insidious wars waged on all we Catholics believe by those within the Church, was through the life-saving Grace of receiving Holy Communion *frequently*. We are told that the Eucharist is Food for the journey. We need this Food to stay on course when the whole world seems to have gone mad.]

The next attack most naturally would be on the *Sacrament of Penance*. Do you ever wonder *why* the enemy always attacks the Eucharist and Penance? Think about it,

the devil and his fallen angels can never ever behold the
Beatific Vision. We can at least on earth, through the
Eucharist, have a foretaste of what a glorious life is ahead
of us in the presence of Our Lord in His glorified state. Then
there is the Sacrament of Penance! The devil and his cohorts
were given *one* chance; God showed them what Heaven
would be like for those who obeyed Him and they chose
Lucifer and eternal damnation. There is no chance of
redemption for them. Jesus gave *us* the Sacrament of
Penance where, through His instruments - His priests,
forgiveness is granted to us over and over again. In addition,
through this Sacrament we are made spotless and pleasing
to Him. The fallen angels are forever ugly, eternally scarred
by the sins they continue to propagate and the disobedience
they breed throughout the world, from that first no to God.

Once again, the Church was at war! What did God do?
What he always does; He raised up an army and this army
brought about a great Revival in the Catholic Church. [One
of our favorite songs is: *"You will know them by their fruits."*]
One of the powerful signs, fruits of the Catholic Revival
was the eagerness the faithful had to be united with Jesus
through frequent Holy Communion.

*"The Church teaches that Holy Communion
separates us from sin. ...the Eucharist cannot unite us
to Christ without at the same time cleansing us from
past sins and preserving us from future sins."*[34]

The Jansenists taught that the Holy Eucharist could *only*
be received by those *worthy* of receiving, and that only
persons with perfect contrition could receive Holy
Communion. Now, as no one is worthy, that really eliminates
everyone. For this reason many followers of Jansen refrained
from receiving Holy Communion for as much as two to three
years at a clip.

As for the Sacrament of Penance, the Jansenists taught

that only those again with *perfect contrition* could receive the Sacrament of Penance. They meted out the most severe penances and the sinner could not receive absolution until all the penances were fulfilled, satisfactorily.

This is a blatant contradiction of all the Church teaches. After having made an examination of conscience, to be absolved of our sins, we need to have contrition (or sorrow) for our sins, to confess with our lips to a priest who has the faculties to forgive sins in the Name of Jesus Christ, and to do satisfaction for our sins by some act of penance prescribed by the priest.

Mother Church further teaches, in the Catechism of the Catholic Church:

"imperfect contrition (or "attrition") is also a gift from God, a prompting of the Holy Spirit. It is born of the consideration of sin's ugliness or the fear of eternal damnation and the penalties threatening the sinner (contrition of fear). Such a stirring of conscience can initiate an interior process which, under the prompting of grace, will be brought to completion by sacramental absolution. By itself however, imperfect contrition cannot obtain the forgiveness of grave sins, but it disposes one to obtain forgiveness in the Sacrament of Penance."[35]

We in the Church say an Act of Contrition whereby we express our sorrow for having sinned, proclaim we detest our sins and firmly resolve to sin no more.

Such an unloving, condemning theology, Jansenism, finally began to fade away at the end of the century, man choosing *The Way, the Truth and the Life Who is Jesus*, He Who died for us on the Cross. Unlike Jansen who made redemption something practically unattainable, Our Lord through His Church reaches out to us, *interceding* with the Father to forgive us, *inviting* us to share life eternal with

Him in the Kingdom.

One man, Michel de Bay (1513-1589) wrote a heretical paper on *Original Sin*, erroneously interpreting St. Augustine. It was condemned by Pope St. Pius V in 1567 and Pope Gregory XIII in 1579. Although condemned, in 1627, Cornelius Jansen used this as reference for the book he was writing, *Augustinus*, allegedly based on St. Augustine's teaching on Grace.

In 1649, a theologian from the highly reputed Sorbonne in Paris, by the name of Nicholas Cornet, wrote a dissertation with five propositions.[36]

The Five Propositions were:

(1) As the grace of God is lacking, some Commandments are impossible even for the just;

(2) interior grace can never be resisted because of our fallen state;

(3) a person does not need freedom from necessity to merit or demerit in the state of a fallen nature;

(4) Semi-Pelagians heretically taught that grace could be accepted or rejected by the human will; and

(5) Christ did not die for all humanity. - Although he insisted they had nothing to do with Jansen's *Augustinus*, and used the name of St. Augustine to give his work credibility, it was plain to everyone that they were definitely influenced by Jansen. Written quite ambiguously, they became nonetheless an issue which caused controversy and future division, some theologians for and the Holy See against.

One man wrote a controversial paper; although it was condemned a second used it; then not waiting upon the decision of the Church, a *third* man published what the second man had written; then a *fourth* man used what the third man had published; and because of the pride of these men who put themselves above the wisdom of the Church, a splinter broke off the Cross of Salvation, dividing and killing, shattering Jesus' Cross in many parts.

It never ended! Although Jansen and his early followers did not want to break away from the Church, his errors would breed dissent upon dissent; the Popes no sooner issuing Bulls condemning the writings of someone proposing Jansenism than new authors would crop up. No sooner was some kind of peace realized than someone else wrote a book confirming Jansen's writings, and that got condemned. Pasquier Quesnel wrote a book: *Réflexions morales*, advocating Jansenism. Endeavoring to keep peace, Pope Clement XI had shown compassion to the Jansenists, allowing them to remain within the Church if they did not promote Jansen's propositions; now he was left with no recourse but to issue a Bull *Unigenitus* condemning *Quesnel's* book containing 101 propositions based on the writings by Jansen that had been condemned. This would lead to more division with most of the French clergy accepting the Bull and the Jansenists refusing to obey the Church.

No sooner - one battle fought and won, then another attack is waged. Despairingly, even after all the Pope's attempts to keep his family together, with concession after concession, the time came when even the clergy stubbornly refused to obey the Church's authority. King Louis XIV was also to use Jansenism at one point, to foster his self-seeking tool of Gallicanism. But he soon tired of all the squabbling and friction which ensued. No longer convenient, the King revoked his former patronage, making it difficult for the Jansenists to preach throughout France, and so they left for more fertile ground.

Next stop for the Jansenists - the Netherlands! The ground work of division had been set for them. The Church in the Netherlands had already been fragmented by schismatics from all sides: From Germany with the

Lutherans, from England with Protestantism, and France with Calvinism. Now the Jansenists entrenched, the Church and the faithful of the Netherlands would suffer another schism! Their apostasizing most zealous, they were able to win to their thinking even one of the Holy See's appointed vicar apostolics.[37] When he began spreading their heresies, Pope

Pope Clement XI

Clement XI had no option but to remove him. In 1723, the Jansenists, now without even a dim memory of their founder's intent to remain within the Church, responded by electing their own bishop. Jansenists kept recruiting many within and without the Church until in 1786, Jansenism was again condemned as a heresy by The Synod of Pistoia. There is an expression: *What part of no don't you understand?*

Heresy always festering under the surface, Jansenism was to rear its ugly head once again. The Church once again is called to make clear its position. We're in the early 1900s, and a new attack is being launched. Some from within and without Mother Church were unwilling to accept the Church's decree on Jansenism; it had resurfaced as a heresy called *Moral Jansenism*. Pope St. Pius X, seeing what one heresy of Modernism was doing to the fiber of the Church, acted swiftly and condemned Jansenism under this new title. It never stopped! But the warriors are on both sides: some for Mother Church and others against her. However, since our General and Commander in Chief is Jesus, we all know to whom the wreath of victory will go.

With the Hearts of Jesus and Mary, I wonder how many of them realized what they were doing, and realize today what they are doing? Sometimes, we get so set on what we judge is right, we cannot back down. Being Catholic, it is one of the decisions in life we find simple to make:

If the Church says it, it is good enough for us!

Gallicanism attacks the Papacy

Of all the attacks on the Faith, this was one of the most malignant, its sick cells spreading, destroying healthy ones in its path. The tumors of division and dissent began to spread, their spores begetting more spores, wildly reproducing, contaminating first France and then most of Catholic Europe. The ills of the Seventeenth Century spilled into the the Eighteenth Century, with the church in France demanding independence from the Papacy. [Are we not hearing the same thing today: We must separate ourselves from the Church in Rome?]

But how did it all start? This cancerous schism first began with the pervading *false god of nationalism* that was so central in the Eighth and Ninth Centuries. Under the title of *Conciliarism*, Gallicanism really raised its ugly head in the Twelfth and Thirteenth Centuries among theologians who were hell-bent on demeaning the authority of the Pope.

Conciliarism was essentially a *heretical* theory falsely addressing the important issue of who possessed supreme authority in the Church. It flatly stated that a general assembly of bishops acting *independently* of the Pope, had the highest power to determine doctrines and correct errors. It further alleged that this power did not belong to the Pope, nor to a genuine ecumenical council.

First, the Church teaches, a general council of bishops, acting independent of the Pope, is not an ecumenical council, and since only an ecumenical council has the power *to* determine or prevent errors, a general assembly is powerless to fulfill the function *Conciliarism* claimed it could.

An ecumenical council is an official assembly of all the bishops of the world, which, when summoned by the Bishop of Rome, the Pope, constitutes the highest teaching authority in the Church.[38]

Christ gave our first Pope, and consequently all who have followed him in perfect unbroken succession, the Keys to the Kingdom (the Church) and as the Keeper the right to use all power of jurisdiction in the Church, even to that of an ecumenical council.

Conciliarism misrepresented the office of the Pope. Unchecked, *Conciliarism* went on to declare that *everyone* who was part of the Christian community, had the responsibility and God-given right to prevent errors, and no one person - not even the Pope had the sole authority to determine what is truth and what is false.

Growing bolder, a theologian pridefully went a step further with a treatise insisting that the Pope, although the steward of God in spiritual and temporal matters, could be removed by those who had elected him, as they represented the wider body of the faithful. [Sounds like a democratic process he is proposing; our Church never has been *a democratic* but from its inception - always *hierarchical*.] This theologian argued that the state should be the final word in not only matters of state but in the affairs and teachings of the Church.

One act of dissidence stealthily grew into another, movements against the Church and the Papacy gaining momentum, until a crisis surfaced in the Fourteenth Century and almost succeeded because it had the French King's support. Sadly not only the monarchy and the court, but many of the clergy found it convenient and self-serving to uproot the authority of the Papacy and put it under the heel of the French general council.[39]

In 1398 the new king - Charles VI, not satisfied with claiming he owed no allegiance to Benedict XIII because he was the anti-pope, wrote an edict proclaiming the French Church independent and separate from Rome. He said that he had based it on certain traditions and rights that he had *supposedly* recently discovered. Furthermore, standing on the legitimacy of *Conciliarism*, he proclaimed a special status for the Church in France, declaring that the general council had greater authority than the Pope and therefore they could depose him, if they so desired. He named his decree: *Libertiés de L'Église gallicane*, after which Gallicanism derived its name.

The battle raged on with King Charles VII in 1438 making further claims that the authority of the Papacy was limited to and restricted by the will of the reigning monarch and valid only if in accord with the conditions of Conciliarism.

Then there was the concordat in 1516 which stated that the Throne reserved the right to choose members of the Church hierarchy.

Gallicanism had its lows and highs until 1600 when it sharply escalated! In 1682, the French Clergy assembled and issued the Four Gallican rights outlining certain privileges for the Church in France. It was condemned by Pope Alexander VIII and then later in 1693, it was withdrawn by the French clergy.

Benedict XIII was the last of the Popes dwelling in Avignon. For 68 years the Popes led the Church from Avignon, having fled from Rome because the Papacy faced danger from the Colonna family who desired to rule Rome. In 1377 Pope Gregory XI returned to Rome.[40] After his death, instead of a French Pope, an Italian Pope Urban VI was elected. The French Cardinals were not too happy about this, accusing the College of Cardinals of having bowed or yielded to Roman pressure. Diplomacy not his strong suit, then Pope Urban VI further alienated them. The French Cardinals, in retaliation, elected anti-pope Clement VII, a Frenchman who took up residence in Avignon.

The Great Western Schism had begun and the Church was split in two. Pope Urban VI died. But the Schism did not die with the death of the Pope, but continued with the Popes who followed: Bonifax IX, Innocent VII, and Gregory XII. Then Clement VIII died in 1394, but that was not to be the end. Another anti-pope - Benedict XIII was elected in Avignon. They had hit an impasse. Neither side would call a general council to resolve the crisis. Finally *Conciliarists*, believing it was the only way, brought about the convening of a council at Pisa. The only problem was that they complicated matters more by electing another anti-pope, Alexander V. Now there was the legitimate Pope in Rome - Gregory XII, the anti-pope in Avignon - Benedict XIII, and another anti-pope in Pisa - Alexander V. Then after his death, Alexander V was followed by another anti-pope, John XXIII.[41] But to give John XXIII credit, it was he who agreed to a council being called to decide the matter. The Council of Constance (1414-1418) was called. Gregory XII resigned; both Benedict XIII and John XXIII were asked to step down, and Martin V was elected;[42] the Church was united under the Seat of Peter in Rome, and the Schism came to an end.

"Vatican Council I condemned Conciliarism. Then Vatican Council II confirmed the collegiality[43] or corporate nature of the episcopate[44] but in so doing it also stressed that such collegiality was not over or superior to the powers of the Papacy. The 1983 Code of Canon Law makes it punishable by censure any attempt to make appeal to an ecumenical council an act or declaration by the Pope."[45]

How did this fire get started and who was responsible

for the fanning of the flames? It always seems to start and end with those most favored by the Lord. Judas was one of the favored twelve and look what he did! Two theologians from the University of Paris - Pierre D'Ailly and Jean (John) Gerson, using their brilliance against the Lord's Pope, began as far back as the Fourteenth Century, to pave the way for the acceptance of this heresy, especially from the hierarchy. Their writings not only defined Gallicanism but gave future Gallicanists fuel for the ongoing fire they were igniting in an attempt to end the Church as we know it.

The Monarchy in France maintained its dominance over the Church in France, holding on to it, dealing whatever blows necessary to keep control of the Church and the following of faithful Frenchmen who did not know they were no longer Catholic. Gallicanism was kept alive and well, to the shame of not only influential members of the court but to the bishops and cardinals who stood to also gain by the disobedience to the Holy See.

But not all the bishops and cardinals supported the state and Gallicanism. *Many* stood by the different orders, trying to protect them, often dying beside them, when they faced torture and execution by King Louis XV and his court. This continued right up to the French Revolution, which gave birth to other persecutors of the Church. With this new brand of oppression and cruelty, the ransacking of churches and monasteries, soldiers using basilicas for stables, the clergy had to make choices again!

The bravery and the loyalty shown by the clergy and their bishops, when the new government wanted them to sign an oath to The Civil Constitution of the Clergy, more than ever justified them their never-dying place in Mother Church's heart as *Eldest Daughter of the Church*. Out of 130 archbishops and bishops, only 4 chose to betray their Church and their vows, and took the Oath. Out of the 70,000 priests, barely 20,000 took the Oath. And when they heard of Pope Pius VI's condemnation of the Oath, *they* turned around and renounced the Oath and disclaimed their former acceptance, many knowing this would cost them their lives. Only our Triune God knows how many martyrs died, rather than deny their Pope and their Church. *Oh Lord, come to your people: clergy, religious and laity alike and fill them with Your Holy Spirit so that we will know a Catholic Revival unrivaled in the history of the Church.*

But many did not know of these loyal members of the Church and the price they paid; only bad news seems to spread. What kings and queens, dukes and duchesses, the selfish and greedy could not do, a priest[46] through his revolution would cause to come to pass. The Protestant Reformation (or Revolution) was responsible for the advance of Gallicanism not only in France but was largely culpable for its success in the rest of Europe, leading to the tragic secularization of many former Catholic countries until today.

Kings and then statesmen never gave up on their ongoing focus (no different from leaders of state today who try to ply our churches and Catholic schools with benefits in an attempt to control them): *Influence the bishops to turn against the Pope!* But the Church fought back! It looked lost there for awhile, but then as the stones could not keep silent and the heart yearns for the Lord our God, so a *Catholic Revival* rose from the ashes and spread throughout the countryside bringing change and hope to the Faithful, strength to those dry martyrs, bishops and priests who had opposed the gallicanization or nationalization of France. As today, then too, strong religious orders stepped forward - Dominicans and Jesuits staunchly opposing this dangerous heresy. As this raised the ire and wrath of the ruling class, they paid with not only their bodies, but some lived to see the final and total repression and persecution of their orders in France.

Gallicanism kept cropping up and being mowed down for several centuries, the Jansenists using it to fight a Papal Bull by Pope Clement XI which condemned 100 Jansenist theological assertions. It was believed that the last shadow of Gallicanism was stamped out by the 1800s, most notably with the declaration of *Papal Infallibility* by the First Vatican Council. But old dogs refuse to die, the bear[47] is not dead but waiting, and Satan never sleeps. What we thought was dead surfaced and resurfaced. As you study Luther you hear him calling for a Church for *Germans*; and then with Calvin you see him successfully going about fragmenting and then destroying all that is Catholic in Switzerland, by beginning a *nationalist* Church in Geneva run by him and the state; and now with certain bishops calling for an American Church in our own century, we see *Gallicanism* alive and threatening God's children once more. But this time it is different. God has a larger army ready to fight the good fight! Gallicanism was dispelled over and over again, only to crop up again. This and other heresies attacked and we the Church fought, ready to fight another fight another day. And now as we anticipate the Church's Jubilee Year of 2000, we say: *Fight we did and fight we will, if need be.*

Footnotes

[1]Although they were descendants of French royalty, there were those Frenchmen who considered them foreigners and were most unhappy when they began to have influence over state affairs in France. They looked upon them as usurpers, gaining power through the merger of Burgundy with France.

[2]The Netherlands is comprised today of Holland, Belgium, and a minuscule part of northern France.

[3]the theater, pamphlets and dissident clergy who masqueraded as part of the Church

[4]Nothing could be farther from the True Teaching of the Church, which teaches that the only way to the Father is through His Son. The value of journeying to Shrines is to get closer to God, in order to understand His plan in our lives; and to give us the resolve, the strength to accept His Will. To ask the intercession of Mary at her Shrines dates back to Jesus' first miracle at Cana when He changed water into wine. His Mother *interceded* for the newly-weds. Visiting the Shrines of the Saints and the Angels is to ask holy friends and family, redeemed by the Blood of the Lamb, to pray for us to the Lord Our God. This tradition was followed by Jesus Himself when He pilgrimaged to Jerusalem, fulfilling the traditions of His ancestors, the Israelites before Him.

[5]politically and geographically

[6]King of the Netherlands

[7]read about these Miracles in Bob and Penny's books: *This is My Body, This is My Blood, Miracles of the Eucharist, Books I & II*

[8]Abraham Lincoln first said this and Franklin D. Roosevelt borrowed it using it in his tenancy as President of the United States.

[9]In the Netherlands, the once predominant Lutheran Church has become so fragmented, there is little or no religion of any kind being practiced by the majority.

[10]at the present time, only Northern Ireland

[11]Mary Queen of Scots

[12]You can read more about this heresy and others in Bob and Penny's book: *Scandal of the Cross and Its Triumph, Heresies throughout the History of the Church.*

[13]Most of the people believed that Mary Stuart was the legitimate heir to the throne, because she was the oldest (and therefore next in line) *legitimate* descendant of an English King-King Henry VII, father of King Henry VIII, and Elizabeth had no legitimate claim to the throne, as she was the *illegitimate* offspring from the invalid marriage of King Henry VIII and Anne Boleyn.

[14]the banner they carried

[15]for more on the many martyrs who gave their lives for the Faith, read

Bob and Penny's book: *Martyrs, They died for Christ.*

[16]Her father King Henry VIII received the treasured title: *Defender of the Faith,* before he demanded the Pope declare his marriage to Catherine of Aragon invalid so that he could marry Anne Boleyn - You can read more on this in the chapter in this book on King Henry VIII.

[17]For more on the many Irish martyrs, as well as those from other nations, who gave their lives for the Faith, read Bob and Penny's book: *Martyrs, They died for Christ.*

[18]Inquire at our office 1-800-633-2484 for videos showing this and more on the Irish Martyrs.

[19]for more on this, read Bob and Penny's book: *Martyrs, They died for Christ.*

[20]Otto I commanded the Pope to crown him emperor. When Pope John did not bow to his will, Otto deposed the Pope, in favor of Leo VIII.

[21]Religious Peace of Augsburg

[22]all in Germany

[23]with a very few exceptions

[24]the Papacy

[25]Gen 18:26

[26]St. Teresa of Avila

[27]Now this priest was only two years a priest, a late vocation, a convert, and an ex-Marine to boot.

[28]French lay volunteers who came with the Jesuits to Canada and upstate New York in the Sixteenth Century. Their stories of martyrdom are included in Bob and Penny's book: *Martyrs, They died for Christ.*

[29]It just goes to show: Some listen and some talk! Archbishop Fulton J. Sheen, a true prophet who predicted these latter days of disobedience and modernism, suffered much persecution during his lifetime because of his insistence on true obedience to the Magisterium. He too, graduated from the University of Louvain.

[30]from The Catholic Church through the Ages - Martin P. Harney, S.J. - St. Paul Editions

[31]In our third book of the Trilogy, we will cover cults that believe in predestination.

[32]known as the *Pope of Frequent Communion*

[33]Read more about this and other heresies from the First Century till today in Bob and Penny's book: *Scandal of the Cross and Its Triumph, Heresies throughout the History of the Church.*

[34]St. Ambrose, Catechism of the Catholic Church #1393

[35]Catechism of the Catholic Church #1453

[36]Catholic History - Our Sunday Visitor

[37]A *vicar apostolic* is a priest or bishop who is under direct orders from the Holy See. He can be over a missionary district where the hierarchy has not been established. His rights and faculties are governed by Canon Law. - Catholic Encyclopedia - Broderick

[38]Catholic History and Dictionary - Our Sunday Visitor

[39]Does this sound like something we have been hearing, that every bishop and then every pastor (under his guidelines) is to decide for himself what the faithful in their parish and diocese will believe, not in what the Papacy directs and the Magisterium teaches? And that my brothers and sisters has to result in the end of the *One, Holy, Catholic, Apostolic Church*, founded by Our Lord Jesus, eternally Universal. And perhaps is this what they are in reality trying to do?

[40]Read more about the return of the Pope to Rome in chapter on Catherine of Siena in Bob and Penny's book: *Saints and other Powerful Women in the Church*.

[41]the anti-pope and not John XIII of Vatican Council II

[42]He was the 1st Pope to *solely* preside in peace, without any anti-popes, in almost thirty-nine strife-filled years of division.

[43]Collegiality means the common responsibility which the whole episcopal body, the bishops, **under the Pope**, has for the evangelization of the world and the establishment of the Church throughout the whole world.

[44]Office, dignity and Sacramental powers bestowed on a bishop at ordination. The Episcopacy is the full group of the hierarchy known as bishops, who acting collegially (in communion with and under obedience to the Pope) are the government of the Church.

[45]Catholic History - Our Sunday Visitor

[46]Martin Luther

[47]as Russia has often been referred to

Reform or Revolution?

So many dead bodies on the road to the Kingdom!
How did the Cross fall apart, after all the pain suffered by
the Lamb of God on the Cross of Sacrifice? Jesus opened
His Arms wide and let man kill Him, loving him till the end.
We love our separated brothers and sisters in Christ and the
Jews of the Old Testament. We pray through the Hearts of
Jesus and Mary Whose *Yes* changed the world that our book
has radiated our love for them, that the Holy Spirit has guided
us to write the truth with love.

Doing research for our book on *Heresies,*[1] we found
ourselves crying, as we saw good men turning away from
the Church which Jesus founded, the one the Holy Spirit
has guided and protected these 2000 years. We find it hard
to believe they understood the harm they were doing and
the chaos that would follow, from their disobedience. How
could they have suspected, as they went about doing what
they thought best, that it would lead to confusion!

*"Enter through the narrow gate; for the gate is wide and
the road broad that leads to destruction, and those who enter
through it are many."*[2] Right from the beginning of the
Church, the father of lies and confusion has been leading
many through that wide gate, that comfortable gate, that no
suffering, no pain, no Cross gate. At the foot of the Cross,
as Jesus was struggling with His last breath, Satan used men
to taunt Jesus into coming down from the Cross; and Satan
has been using people ever since to take Jesus down from
the Cross so that His children, no longer seeing the price He
willingly paid, will not pick up their cross and follow Him.

How did it all happen?

As we look at our Church and what has been happening, our thoughts go back to the Vatican and Michelangelo's Pieta. We can see the statue, Mother Mary holding her Son, limp in her arms and the look on her face. Looking up to Heaven, she looked as if she was saying, "Was this what I agreed to when I said `Let it be done unto me according to Your Word?'" But to the end, she obeyed the Father's Will. What has she done to offend so many?

One day, a crazed young man began striking at the statue of the Blessed Mother. They stopped him, but it was too late; Mother Mary had suffered the blows, her nose chipped and her beautiful face almost crushed. The statue was repaired, but the scars remain. The attack had not been on her Son, but on His Mother. She had sustained the blows she could not take away from her Son on the Cross. But the statue was not destroyed, no more than Jesus will allow her or the Church, of which she is Mother, to be destroyed.

There have been so many lies sown that the lies have become for some, the truth. This is why we would like to share the Calendar of Events and a little background on what some of the splinters that split from our Church, believe. This is a call for those splinters who broke off from the Cross of Jesus Christ to come Home; we love you.

✝ ✝ ✝

33 A.D. - The Roman Catholic Church

The Roman Catholic Church was founded by Jesus Christ. Through the unbroken succession of Popes and Apostles beginning with our first Pope and Apostle - Peter, this same Church is in existence till today.

**The History of those who left Mother Church
Main-Line Protestant Denominations** considered
Christians.

1457 - The Moravians

Tracing their history back to John Hus, they consider
themselves the oldest Protestant denomination. They greatly
influenced John Wesley the founder of the Methodists.
Shortly after Hus' death they formed *Unitas Fratrum* or
Unity of the Brethren. By the end of the Sixteenth Century,
it had become the largest Protestant church in Bohemia until
the *Thirty Years War* scattered the members. They believe
in the Apostles Creed, but *mystically* rather than as a
profession of faith. They believe much like the Evangelical
Lutherans with one exception; they have a special devotion
to Christ Crucified and His most precious Wounds.

They have no altars, do not believe in baptizing infants,
and only celebrate *the Lord's Supper*[3] six or seven times a
year. They receive bread and wine *standing* after they shake
hands with each other. As communion is only a *symbol* in
their church, other Christians are welcome to participate in
their services.[4] They allow children to receive communion,
only after having been Confirmed. The have what they call
the *Love Feast* where they share coffee and sweet rolls.

In the beginning, they drew lots before making
important decisions: who would go on missions, when and
where they would go to evangelize, who would marry whom
and when, which laws were to be passed, etc. This practice
fell into misuse and was terminated in the Nineteenth
Century. Today Moravian membership totals more than
300,000 worldwide.[5]

1517 - The Lutheran Denominations

The Lutheran Denominations originated when Martin
Luther rebelled against the authority of the Pope and broke
from the Roman Catholic Church in 1517.[6]

Sixteenth Century - The Mennonites - formerly Anabaptists

As Luther and Calvin broke from the Catholic Church, so the **Anabaptists** broke from the Lutheran Church. Refusing to obey *the Lutheran theology*, they were branded heretics, and started their own church. Preaching *non-violence*, they- would not take up arms, and were persecuted by the state. They chose their ministers, untrained and unpaid, by drawing lots. They saw themselves as a community of brotherhood, all equal, no headship. They would not take any oaths and were not allowed to run for public office.

The **Mennonites,** originally a splinter from the Anabaptists, claim they date back to the 1520s, and began in Central Europe. *Menno Simons*, who had been a Catholic priest for twelve years when he decided to join the Anabaptists, was the force which would make them into another denomination. He organized them and introduced some of the theology he maintained from the Catholic Church. With his strong leadership he drew many to him and a *new* religion! For this reason, they took his name.

Concerns over sound theology, the Sacraments or liturgy, have never been their focus, which is to live *"godly lives,"* separate from people who are not Mennonites. They also refuse to take up arms, vote or hold public office. They wear somber, often black, austerely plain clothes dating back to the dress of their ancestors. They marry within their own church and closely control their families' formation, molding them into *a tight society*.

Their doctrine declares: *"That mixed marriages between believers and non-believers are unscriptural, and marriage with divorced persons with former companions living constitute adultery."* They, like the Anabaptists, do not believe in wearing worldly clothes, engaging in warfare, the swearing of oaths, or joining secret societies.[7]

The **Amish** broke away from the Mennonites in 1693. Their motto is *"The old is best and the new is of the devil."* They shun *backsliders*, legislate a standard dress code, do not believe in education past the elementary grammar school level, worship in homes and barns as opposed to worshiping in churches like other Christians. They insist on marrying within the Amish communities,[8] and deem it essential their children practice the Amish Faith. Like most Mennonites the Amish are proficient farmers - although they do not believe in using modern implements. They are baptized in their late teens. They are not allowed to use electricity, telephones, central heating, automobiles [Visiting Pennsylvania, we have seen them driving their quaint black horse-drawn carriages], tractors and etc. Some very strict Amish communities prohibit the use of mirrors, colorful or silk clothing, pressed trousers and photographs - Calvinism to the extreme. Others separated from the Amish and formed a Mennonite Conference - another splinter. This is what happens when *man found*s *a faith* and not Jesus.

1534 - The Church of England

The Church of England separated from the Roman Catholic Church in 1534, when the Pope refused to sanction King Henry VIII's divorce, and he declared himself head of the Church in England.[9]

Seventeenth Century
The Protestant Episcopalian Church

At the outbreak of the American Revolution, most Anglican clergy fled to England, since they had all taken an oath of loyalty to the King. Without pastors, the colonists chose Samuel Seabury to be their bishop. He tried for one year in England, to be consecrated, but as he was not a British subject, it was to no avail. He turned to the fugitive Scottish Episcopal Church and was finally consecrated as a bishop in 1784. He returned to America and founded the Episcopal

Church. It did not do well, as its roots were English and it was no match for the zealous Methodist and Baptist preachers who were drawing pilgrims to *their* churches.

Here in the United States, they have adopted their own *American* version of the Book of Common Prayer. They accept the Apostles Creed and Nicene Creed as *symbols* of the Faith and a modified version of the original thirty-nine articles[10] as a *general* statement of doctrine. But now with the introduction of women as clergy, bishops, priests and deacons, the good news is that Episcopalians, and Anglicans - priests and whole congregations, are coming back Home to the Roman Catholic Church.

1560 - The Presbyterian Church

The Presbyterian Church was founded by John Knox, originally a follower of John Calvin. In the year 1560, proclaiming himself a prophet, Knox left the Calvinists and started his own religion, taking with him followers discontented with Calvin. Again, based on whom you ask, will you find answers to what this fragment of the Truth believes. There are those who believe in *Predestination*, as their ancestors before them and those who are told they can take or leave it, by their pastors. Offshoots of the original Presbyterian Church are: U.S. Cumberland Presbyterian or United Presbyterian.

Early Seventeenth Century
The Congregationalist Church
(later merged and became **United Church of Christ**)

Wanting to separate from the Church of England, they first went to Holland. That proving unsuccessful, they returned to England but soon left for the New World on the Mayflower. This was the Religion of the *Pilgrims* who landed in New England. Although fleeing from religious persecution, they proved to be equally intolerant of other religions.

1605 - The Baptist Church

The Baptist Church was begun in Amsterdam in 1605 by John Smyth who had originally been ordained in the Church of England. In 1608, he put together the basic beliefs of his new church, and later recanted[11] all he had written and tried to enter the Mennonites. His followers left for England and established what we know today as the Baptist Religion.

Baptists believe in *Justification through faith alone.* They do not believe that Baptism is a Sacrament. They did away with all creeds, infant baptism, all seven Sacraments, all formalized liturgies. They believe as we do, in the *Holy Trinity,* the *Virgin Birth*, that *Jesus Christ is Divine*, in *His Incarnation*, in *Jesus' redemption of man on the Cross*, in *Original Sin*, in *Heaven and hell*.[12] They believe strongly in the infallibility of the Bible where it suits their agenda.

In many ways the Baptists are closer to us in beliefs than other Protestant denominations. The sad truth is that many have bought into so many lies and fables espoused by ignorant or fallen-away Catholics on what Catholicism is, there is often a suspicion and a hatred directed at Catholics by these brothers and sisters whom we love so dearly. A big difference is there is no universality, as there is in the Catholic Church, because they have no head, no bishop who makes them one united family believing in one Truth. Each church is self-governed by elders, hiring and firing their minister at whim.

1649 - The Quakers - The Religious Society of Friends

As with Luther and Wesley, George Fox, the founder of the Quakers, had no intention of forming a new church. As his family had little resources to send him to school, and as at twelve years of age, he had to serve as an apprentice to a shoemaker, he had little or no education. He became disenchanted with his church when he witnessed two clergymen behaving badly under the influence of alcohol.

He claimed he had a vision where God spoke to him. He left his family, church, friends and wandered around England for four years. He came to the conclusion that man does not discover the truth by studying, reading the Bible, attending services and hearing sermons, but through an *Inner Light* through which God speaks to each soul. He gathered those who were disenchanted with the Anglicans and others who looked critically upon Calvinism and its severity. He attracted pseudo-mystics who were attracted to this personal mystical encounter with God.

The Quakers do not practice any of the traditional outward forms of Christianity, including Sacraments. They do not believe in rituals of any kind in their church. There is no preaching, only silence until per chance one of the assembly is inspired and shares a religious insight. With the compromises that are taking place in even this denomination, that has been somewhat modified with some churches having a silent time after their vocal meetings. One of the beliefs so difficult to accept is that they do not believe that anyone, not even God, can atone for another's sins. They highly esteem the Bible but as *a* word of God, not *the* Word of God. Since they do not accept any ritual, Baptism and the Lord's Supper is rejected.

1744 - The Methodist Church *"All the world is My parish."*

This was John Wesley's answer to those who questioned his right to preach. The Methodist Church was founded in England in 1744, by Wesley, a former Priest in the Church of England. Like so many of the original schisms[13] from the Catholic Church, there are many similarities between the Methodist practices and those of the Catholic Faith.

When it looked as if the Church of England was waning, two of its members, disenchanted with the Church of their father, became the catalysts which would bring about the birth of another religion, *Methodism*. Although it was not well accepted in Oxford University where it began, it has evolved into the second largest Protestant religion in the United States, claiming 13 million followers in the United States and 18 million in the four corners of the world.

When they suffered ridicule, because they believed in frequent reception of communion, fasting on Wednesdays and Fridays, spending two hours praying and reading the Bible, John Wesley and his brother Charles, along with other students went out and preached and prayed with the poor and dejected - in prisons, in shacks, in the worst slums - reaching out to everyone abandoned and rejected by society, bringing hope to the forlorn and succor to the helpless.

The brothers set out for the New World to preach to the Indians. Their enthusiasm soon turned into disillusionment, as the Indians failed to accept their teaching on the Gospel. When you compound that with John having some unfortunate love affairs and then being charged of impropriety by a jury of church elders because he insisted everyone go to confession before reception of holy communion,[14] John and his brother were soon on their way back to England. They experienced more disillusionment in London. But then remembering the spirituality they had witnessed in some Moravians, they began to preach anew in the Anglican Church believing it would bring new life. They were shot down, and so they once again took to the streets and the fields. The interesting thing was that Wesley's intention was not to cause another splinter of the Cross to fall off Jesus' Cross. He was not about founding a new denomination. He told everyone to go back to their own churches and be a light which would bring about a revival in the Anglican Church.

Wesley was short on theology, stressing more a horizontal outreach to his fellow men, the Gospel in action, so to speak. The only thing the Methodists emphasized was *man's free will.* Wesley taught that the perfection of man was possible on earth and once having received this sanctification, he would be assured of his place in Heaven. He also believed, although he did not boast of this for himself, that having reached this perfection one would lose all inclination to do evil.

Those who criticized John Wesley and questioned his authority, had to ask themselves how *they* had failed the faithful, for if there had not been a need he would not have had an audience.

Twentieth Century - The Pentecostal Church

This is a movement, rather than a sect, made up of many little churches, each one autonomous, run individually by its pastor, without guidance or supervision, leaving them devoid of any kind of unity, ignoring Jesus prayer to the Father, *"that they may all be one, as You Father, are in Me and I in You, that they also may be in Us, that the world may believe that You sent Me."*[15]

They attract Catholics and Protestants uneducated in their own Faith, those who do not know the beauty of their own Church and are attracted to the passion and excitement that is shared at the services in the Pentecostal churches. Something common to most of them is singing, outward demonstrations, clapping of hands and swaying back and forth in the Spirit; the whole experience highly charged, many find it exciting and come back for more. Their very charismatic often dynamic preaching appeals to the vulnerable and to Hispanics who are by nature passionate. *Their Doctrine:*

In reference to **the Bible**: Following the lead of Luther, Calvin and those who followed, Pentecostals believe in *sola scriptura.*[16] But most of their pastors interpret what the Scriptures are saying, and many without theological training have little idea what the Scriptures are really saying. Then there is the strictly Fundamentalist interpretation, which fails to consider the time, the people and the circumstances under which the passages were written. This is not to say that the Lord is not speaking to His people today and for all times; but if we take the Word *literally*, without the guidance of the Church who selected the books and Gospel passages in the first place, we can become confused, and we have another splinter of the True Cross.

Though there are different opinions within the Pentecostals, they all believe and espouse that **being Baptized in the Holy Spirit** is when one receives the gifts of the Holy Spirit, and the sign that one has received the Holy Spirit is receiving the *gift of tongues* or *glossolalia*. Pentecostals say that the other gifts were received from the Holy Spirit before Pentecost.

Another accepted belief is the **gift of prophecy**. The prophecy must be of a happening that will, and does come to pass in the future, with the added condition that it occurs exactly as the prophetic word has been extolled. [With so many people starving for guidance, this can become an abuse, with some using this gift as a kind of holy fortune cookie, moving and acting only on that word they receive at a prayer meeting.]

Another important sign for Pentecostals is *the gift of healing*. Again this can be dangerous; there have been devastating cases when someone has been cured from Cancer, everyone in the church praises God; but when the Cancer returns the congregation turns to the suffering soul and says *"If you had enough faith you would still be healed."* When we heard this we were furious! Imagine, if the pain of having the Cancer returns and the prospects of leaving loved ones, is not debilitating enough, to add a lack of faith to the burden this poor soul is carrying is nothing short of cruelty.

Do some people have a **gift of healing**? We have no doubt! It's Scriptural. But our priests have that gift through the Sacrament of Holy Orders, when they bless us. Jesus is the *ultimate* Healer, and we Catholics believe He comes to us during the Mass in the Holy Eucharist and that He can and will heal us, if we ask and it is best for the salvation of our soul. Then when we are kneeling before the Blessed Sacrament whether at Mass or adoring Him in the Tabernacle or in the Monstrance, our Lord is present. Why do we depend on man; why not speak to our Lord; He hears us; He loves us; He wants to heal us.

Pentecostals have different **beliefs in the Holy Trinity**, with some believing as we do that the Holy Trinity consists of One God in three Persons - *the Father, the Son,* and *the Holy Spirit*, and an essential part of *Baptism* is invoking the Holy Trinity. Others differing with them and us, only believe that Baptism comes about in and through *Jesus Christ alone*. Their concept of the Trinity is: There are not really three Persons in the One God, but that the Father is *Christ* in the Old Testament and the Holy Spirit is *Christ* after Pentecost; therefore there is only *Christ*, the God Who shed His Blood on the Cross. This would make them a **cult**, for to be considered a Christian, one must believe in the *Triune God*.

How do they feel about Mary? One of the big dividing lines has been Mother Mary! They believe that Mary was a virgin when she conceived Jesus in her womb. On this we agree; but they also believe, as many Protestants do, that Mother Mary had other children after Jesus. Now this is not even in the equation. Maybe our biggest argument is at the foot of the Cross: Jesus is laboring to speak; He is close to death; His words are bought at the cost of excruciating pain and suffering. Part of those last precious words were Jesus leaving His Mother to John! If there had been other brothers and sisters, this would have been a grave insult. According to the Jewish tradition, as family, they would be the ones who would care for their Mother.

Pentecostals do not consider **Our Lady an intercessor**. Now they will pray for one another. They ask sinners[17] to pray for them, their loved ones, or any one of a million petitions, but not His Mother Who is in Heaven. *Does this make sense?* Jesus' first Miracle was through His Mother's intercession at Cana, when He changed water into wine at her request. When Jesus performed that Miracle was he not assuring us we could turn to His Mother, the way the wedding party did, and He would help us? Isn't it interesting, how Jesus' *first* Miracle, His first act was through His Mother and His last act was to give us His Mother? If we belittle Mary's role in our lives, we wound Jesus, her Son!

Do they **believe in the Eucharist**? They celebrate the Lord's Supper, *symbolically* - believing the Eucharist is merely a symbol; they do not believe, as we do, in the *Real Presence* of Jesus in *His Body, Blood, Soul and Divinity*. They believe The Lord's Supper principally represents:
(a) participation in the Divine Nature of Jesus,
(b) a memorial of His Death and suffering; and
(c) a prophecy of His Second Coming.

They have a devotion to the Blood of Christ and often plead his precious Blood, imploring His protection.

They justify their **proselytism** by their firm conviction theirs is the only good sect, through which someone can be saved. Although they are not in the same league as those very destructive Cults - Jehovah Witnesses and Mormons, to mention just a few, they can lead people astray with their simplistic view of Holy Scripture and their narrow concept of the Word through their fundamentalism.

If there is one quality that has drawn many Catholics to the Pentecostal churches, it is their services are alive with singing and praising the Lord, invoking the Holy Spirit and the fellowship of people loving one another. There is an electricity that generates in the room, and it is infectious! But even as their preachers have said, the feelings go and the people are back the following prayer meeting looking for another high; but the use of the gifts to serve the poor is not part of their message. They act like a holy filling station, but like most highs lacking substance, the high comes requiring more, and not getting more, crashes. With religion, it often results in people joining cults or turning off God altogether.

As for their **belief in the Holy Spirit**, they teach that the Spirit came at Pentecost and then did not come again until the Twentieth Century - through them! To think of God in those terms, either limits Him, or reduces Him to an unloving, uninvolved God Who came and then left His Church to fend for itself for nineteen hundred years - alone, without Him, thus giving *man* the credit for His Church surviving all the attacks, heresies and schisms down through the centuries, from within and without.

✝ ✝ ✝

For us, with their positives and their negatives, our brothers and sisters in Christ have given us a greater appreciation of our Catholic Church and her Treasures, and an urgency to pass on these Treasures to the whole world, to tell them Jesus loves them; Jesus needs them; Jesus is inviting them to be part of His Church. Our Pope, as the Popes before him, is calling the children of God to become one:

"To reunite all his children, scattered and led astray by sin, the Father willed to call the whole of humanity together into his Son's Church. The Church is the place where humanity must rediscover its unity and salvation. The Church is 'the world reconciled.' She is that bark which 'in the full sail of the Lord's cross, by the breath of the Holy

Spirit, navigates safely in this world.' According to another image dear to the Church Fathers, she is prefigured by Noah's ark, which alone saves from the flood. "[18]

Glorify My Name throughout the world!

When we began writing about the *Treasures of the Catholic Church*,[19] we found ourselves crying out to our separated brothers and sisters, that this is what we *all* believed prior to the Sixteenth Century, to shout from the rooftops, from the highest mountains, come Home; this is your inheritance; do not let anyone take it away from you; you deserve this Church; she is your mother, just as she is ours. God the Father sent His only begotten Son and through His Incarnation, we became Jesus' brothers and sisters. On the Cross, Jesus gave His Mother, to you and us! We do not want to keep these Treasures to ourselves; we want to share them with you.

One night I had a dream. I saw people sitting around a round table, arguing with each other. As they attacked each other, there were other people attacking *them* from behind, picking them off, killing them one at a time.

Now is not the time for division and disunity. The enemies of Christ are devious and well-organized! They are, like their leader-*the father of lies*,[20] never asleep. We are endeavoring, with this Trilogy, to beg our brothers and sisters to read how it all came about and put aside our differences and become once again the family that was created at the foot of the Cross. This is for those who have left and do not know what they have left and those who remain and do not know why they remain. It is also for those who are tempted to leave Mother Church, not knowing *all* and *Whom* they are leaving.

Jesus told us, He would not leave us orphans, that He would be with us till the end of the world. Although we can stand on His Word and His Grace is enough for us, the way God has always worked down through the centuries, is by using humans like you and me to touch His children, and bring His Truth to them, leading them to holiness.

Jesus is the Way, the Truth and the Life

Footnotes

[1] *Scandal of the Cross and Its Triumph; Heresies throughout the History of the Church*

[2] Mt 17:13

[3] in Protestant churches a memorial service, where the congregation receives communion as a symbol.

[4] Unlike the Roman Catholic Church, where only Catholics in a state of Grace are allowed to receive Holy Communion, as we believe Our Lord is truly present in the Eucharist.

[5] More in chapter on Wycliff and Hus

[6] More on Luther in chapter on Luther

[7] The Mennonites - *Separated Brethren*, William J. Whalen

[8] but that excludes backsliders

[9] More about the Church of England in chapter on *Henry VIII* in this book.

[10] from Queen Elizabeth

[11] declared it all to be in error

[12] but not Purgatory

[13] Schism-The action of one who voluntarily separates himself from the Church through refusal to submit to the authority of the Church or the Pope and forms another sect. Catholic Catechism-Broderick

[14] a result of his strong High Anglican Church roots

[15] Jn 17:21

[16] believe only that which can be found in the Bible

[17] Everyone who is not in Heaven is a sinner on his journey to Heaven and Sainthood.

[18] Catechism of the Catholic Church #845

[19] Book I of this Trilogy

[20] the devil

Index

Bibliography

Broderick, Robert C. - *The Catholic Encyclopedia*
    Thomas Nelson Inc. Publishers Nashville TN 1970
Harney, Martin P. SJ - *The Catholic Church through the Ages*
    St. Paul Editions - Boston, MA 1974
Belloc, Hilaire - *How the Reformation Happened*
    Tan Books & Publishers, Rockford IL 1992
Belloc, Hilaire - *Characters of the Reformation*
    Tan Books & Publishers, Rockford IL 1992
New Catholic Encyclopedia - 18 Volumes
    Catholic University of America - Washington, DC 1967
O'Hare, Patrick Msgr - *The Facts about Luther*
    Tan Books & Publishers, Rockford, IL 1987
Catholic Encyclopedia & Dictionary - 1994
Encyclopedia of Catholic History - 1995
    Our Sunday Visitor CD Rom
Lord, Bob & Penny -
    This Is My Body, This Is My Blood, Book I - 1986
    The Many Faces of Mary - 1987
    We Came Back to Jesus - 1988
    Saints and Other Powerful Women in the Church - 1989
    Saints and Other Powerful Men in the Church - 1990
    Scandal of the Cross and Its Triumph - 1992
    Martyrs, They Died for Christ 1993
    The Rosary, the Life of Jesus and Mary - 1993
    Visionaries, Mystics and Stigmatists - 1995
    Visions of Heaven, Hell and Purgatory - 1996
Vilar, Juan Diaz SJ - *Religious Sects*
    Catholic Book Publishing Co. - NY 1992
Whalen, William J - *Separated Brethren*
    Our Sunday Visitor - Huntington, IN 1979

Journeys of Faith®

To Order: 1-800-633-2484 FAX 916-853-0132 E-mail BPLord23@aol.com

Books

Bob and Penny Lord are authors of best sellers:

This Is My Body, This Is My Blood;
Miracles of the Eucharist Book I $9.95 Pb
This Is My Body, This Is My Blood;
Miracles of the Eucharist Book II $13.95 Pb
The Many Faces Of Mary, A Love Story $9.95 Paperback $13.95 Hc
We Came Back To Jesus $9.95 Paperback $13.95 Hc
Saints and Other Powerful Women in the Church $13.95 Pb
Saints and Other Powerful Men in the Church $14.95 Pb
Heavenly Army of Angels $13.95 Pb
Scandal of the Cross and Its Triumph $13.95 Pab
The Rosary - The Life of Jesus and Mary $13.95 Hc
Martyrs - They Died for Christ $13.95 Pb
Visionaries, Mystics, and Stigmatists $13.95 Pb
Visions of Heaven, Hell and Purgatory $13.95 Pb
Treasures of the Church - That which makes us Catholic $9.95 Pb
Tragedy of the Reformation $9.95 Pb
Cults - Battle of the Angels $9.95 Pb
Trilogy (3 Books - Treasure..., Tragedy... and Cults...) $25.00 Pb

Please add $4.00 S&H for first book: $1.00 each add'l book

Videos and On-site Documentaries

Bob and Penny's Video Series based on their books:
A 13 part series on the Miracles of the Eucharist - filmed on-site
A 15 part series on The Many Faces of Mary - filmed on-site
A 23 part series on Martyrs - They Died for Christ - filmed on-site
A 10 part series on Saints and Other Powerful Women in the Church
A 12 part series on Saints and Other Powerful Men in the Church
A 14 part series on Visionaries, Mystics and Stigmatists
Many other on-site Documentaries based on Miracles of the Eucharist, Mother
Mary's Apparitions, and the Heavenly Army of Angels. Request our list.
Our books and videos are available in Spanish also

Pilgrimages

Bob and Penny Lord's ministry take out Pilgrimages to the Shrines of Europe, and
Mexico every year. Come and join them on one of these special Retreat Pilgrimages. Call
for more information, and ask for the latest pilgrimage brochure. Call 1-888-262-5673.

Lecture Series

Bob and Penny travel to all parts of the world to spread the Good News. They speak on what
they have written about in their books. If you would like to have them come to your area,
call for information on a lecture series in your area. Call 1-800-633-2484.

Good Newsletter

We are publishers of the Good Newsletter, which is published four times a year. This
newsletter will provide timely articles on our Faith, plus keep you informed with the
activities of our community. Call 1-800-633-2484 for information.